twinkle's weekend knits

twinkle's

20 FAST DESIGNS

weekend

FOR FUN GETAWAYS

knits

WENLAN CHIA

POTTER
CRAFT

NEW YORK

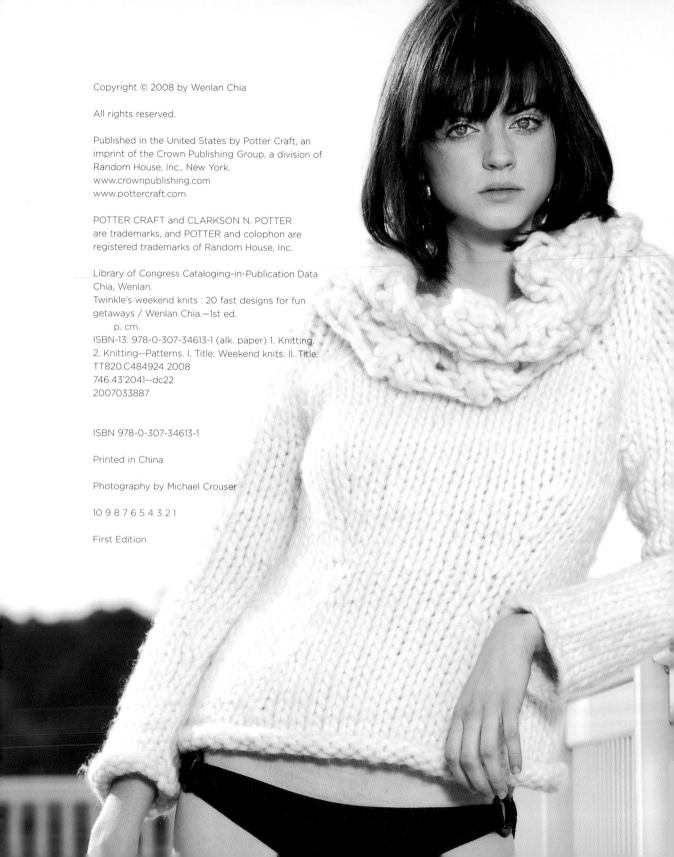

Published in the United States by Potter Craft, an
imprint of the Crown Publishing Group, a division of
Random House, Inc., New York.
www.crownpublishing.com
www.pottercraft.com

POTTER CRAFT and CLARKSON N. POTTER
are trademarks, and POTTER and colophon are
registered trademarks of Random House, Inc.

Library of Congress Cataloging-in-Publication Data
Chia, Wenlan.
Twinkle's weekend knits : 20 fast designs for fun
getaways / Wenlan Chia.—1st ed.
    p. cm.
ISBN-13: 978-0-307-34613-1 (alk. paper) 1. Knitting.
2. Knitting--Patterns. I. Title: Weekend knits. II. Title.
TT820.C484924 2008
746.43'2041--dc22
2007033887

ISBN 978-0-307-34613-1

Printed in China

Photography by Michael Crouser

10 9 8 7 6 5 4 3 2 1

First Edition

ACKNOWLEDGMENTS

*To my parents, Hungyeh Chia and Chuyin Chia,
and my husband, Bernard Lin,
who inspire me to live the creative life that I so enjoy.*

I want to thank all the people who have given of their talent, passion, and heart for every aspect of making this book.

First, thanks to all the people at Potter Craft, who have given me their complete trust and support, especially Rosy Ngo and Erin Slonaker.

Thanks to Caroline Greeven of the Agency Group for always being there when I needed help.

I appreciate Edie Eckman's extreme patience and superb knowledge of knitting.

Thanks to Classic Elite Yarns for their wonderful support, especially Pat Chew, Betsy Perry, and Pam Allen.

Thanks to Charlotte Quiggle for working under difficult deadlines and still managing to do a great job.

My deepest appreciation goes to those who took part in the intense four-day photo shoot and made the trip the most wonderful memory of making this book.

Thanks to Michael Crouser for his talent, patience, and nonstop pursuit of perfection; to Sharon Anderson for being the greatest inspiration for me throughout all my artistic processes in and beyond this book; to John Haffner Layden for giving his modern, Renaissance-man quality from the beginning of this project to its conclusion; to Sara Gelman and David Cruz for creating the models' amazing makeup and hair and for making it look so effortless; to Martina Correa, Ciara Nugent, and Hanne Gaby Odiele, who gave these pictures their brightest smiles and their most beautiful poses; and to Leon Singleton and Soobin Sunwoo for working tirelessly and passionately on every detail.

Thanks to Suzanne Quinn of Glow Communications and to Jessica Longshore of NARS for their continuous support. Thanks to Roger and Mauricio Padilha of MAO for once again doing a great job. Kris Percival and Christie Haffner also deserve my gratitude for applying their keen eyes and knitting know-how to reviewing the book manuscript.

Thanks also go to my amazing staff involved in this book—Katherine Lum, Yuki Sekiya, Karina Peng, Huang Ruixiang, and Lily Tran—for their countless efforts and talents extended to me and to the project. Thanks to my fantastic interns Crystal Wei and Annie Kao for shooing away all the troubles!

Richard Chang and Tina Lee deserve thanks for generously lending their beautiful home for the photo shoot. Thanks also go to the management offices and the staff of the Sands Point Reserve, the Port Washington Yacht Club, the Belmont Lake State Park, the Baxter Estates Pond, and the Baltimore Design Group of Sands Point for allowing us to photograph in these beautiful places.

CREDITS

STYLIST Sharon Anderson
PHOTOGRAPHER Michael Crouser
WRITER AND EDITORIAL CONSULTANT John Haffner Layden
INSTRUCTION WRITER Edie Eckman
TECHNICAL EDITOR Charlotte Quiggle
MAKEUP ARTIST Sara Gelman for NARS
HAIR STYLIST David Cruz for REDKEN
MODELS Martina Correa, Ciara Nugent, and Hanne Gaby Odiele
CASTING MAO PR
SPECIAL CAMEO Milan

CONTENTS

FOREWORD 12

INTRODUCTION 14

1. FRIDAY NIGHT — TWINKLE THROUGH THE NIGHT 18

Boysenberry Scarf 20

Wisteria Scarf 22

Horizon Tunic 24

Nightfall Cropped Top 26

Lilac Mist Throw 28

Sand Dune Hanger Covers 30

2. SATURDAY MORNING — FUN ALFRESCO 32

Snowcap Hat 34

Peony Scarf 34

Borealis Sweater 36

Tidepool Sweater 38

Oceania Sweater 38

Equator iPod Sleeves 38

Northern Cross Sweater 40

Urchin Beret 40

3. SUNDAY AFTERNOON — LAST NIGHT AWAY 42

Nimbus Sweater 44

Autumn Vines Scarf 46

Riverbed Shawl 48

Arbor Row Scarf 50

Cloudburst Cardigan 52

Meridian Tunic Dress 54

TWINKLE TIPS 56

PATTERNS 66

RESOURCES AND YARN SUBSTITUTION 125

INDEX 127

FOREWORD

Weekend living is all about ease, relaxation, rejuvenation, and, most importantly, a time out to dream, create, and—if you are up to the challenge—knit.

In the world of fashion, where one lives for style and often longs for comfort, knits are there to wrap and adorn you—they are the fashion equivalent of comfort food. Knitting them yourself only adds to the pleasure.

Knitting is the ultimate weekend escape. . . . It provides an outlet for creative expression, a time to reflect, and yet you have something wonderful to show for it. Whether you are knitting a breezy tank top for the beach, a heavy chunky knit for the first chill of fall, a cozy throw to curl up in on those snowy winter days, or a brightly colored scarf to walk boldly into spring, *Twinkle's Weekend Knits* has you covered.

For those of you who loved *Twinkle's Big City Knits*, Wenlan Chia lets you leave the city behind with her new book, *Twinkle's Weekend Knits*. Within these pages you will find a world of knits that take you from Friday nights through to Sunday afternoons and beyond. You will twinkle through any weekend in her whimsical knits, which offer a magical adventure wherever you get away.

Have fun, enjoy . . . and keep knitting!!

Fern Mallis

Senior Vice President, IMG Fashion

Organizer of Fashion Weeks in New York, Los Angeles, Miami, and worldwide

INTRODUCTION

I like to think that what you're holding is more than a mere knitting book. Please consider *Twinkle's Weekend Knits* an invitation to escape! Think of it as a "get-out-of-the-daily-grind-free" pass. As a fellow knitter, you know that our craft is perhaps the best antidote to the frenzied pace of contemporary life. But as a fellow member of the modern world, you also know that work, family, and home responsibilities can crowd out time with your beloved needles and yarn. So will you join me on a knitting weekend away to relax, have fun, and reconnect with loved ones? It doesn't have to be a literal getaway; you can hole up in your home and turn off the phone ringer if you prefer. Just let your work ethic lapse, choose some lucky companions, and pack your knitting kit. Cozy up to these quick-knit patterns that you can complete in hours or over a weekend and still have time for some fireside reading and mulled wine or strolling through a park with your pooch. You'll return from our little retreat with color in your cheeks and something warm and woolly around your shoulders.

This book is for the knitter in search of fetching designs to make and wear or give as gifts. It's also for those seeking inspiration from a designer who, over the years, has liberated knitwear from its sometimes unfashionable ancestry! With *Twinkle's Weekend Knits,* I'm sharing some chic, comfy, and sexy designs that have been the foundation of my collections for the Twinkle by Wenlan label.

I've divided the patterns into chapters based on the activities and moods of our mythical weekend away. Let me elaborate. First, close your eyes. Imagine it's Friday, and your workday draws to a close. Moods soften, to-do lists dissolve, and your mind turns away from the weekly routine. Picture yourself settling into a plus club chair in a cozy little nightspot for dinner or drinks with friends. Nice, right? The designs in the first chapter reflect the mood of the end-of-the-workweek knitter—they are some of the simplest patterns, rendered in sophisticated shades that are perfect for casually chic going-out occasions. Here, the versatility of Twinkle designs really shines. When combined with the other garments you packed for the weekend, the pieces in this chapter can elevate the fashion factor or temper the couture quotient as needed for the affair. A fringed scarf with bobbles can usher a dressy skirt into a charming country inn, while a flirty top can ratchet up the glam of a plain skirt. In short, these knits put the fun back in social functions.

By Saturday morning, thoughts of your favorite yoga class, sailing conditions, and dinner menu ideas top your priority list. The blackberries you're keeping close by are the ones destined for pie, not the electronic variety tethering you to the office. The second chapter takes its colors, patterns, and moods from that burst of energy one gets after a refreshing night away. Sprightly silhouettes and colors unite this chapter, whose designs are a little more complex and require a bit more time and concentration.

As the end of our weekend escape nears, you're rejuvenated and savoring those final moments away. There's just enough time to unwind on a sylvan path and then unwind a skein of maize-colored chunky wool by the fireplace. The muted hues of the designs echo the tranquil tone of the Sunday Afternoon chapter.

Perusing the photographs in *Twinkle's Weekend Knits* will give you a window into the Twinkle mode of styling. By now you've probably noticed that my distinctive fashion point of view is one of whimsy, wit, and freshness. Essential to creating the flattering and feminine Twinkle look are some favorite knit techniques, such as ribbed knits and short-row shaping to tailor contours for flattering silhouettes; circular-needle knitting for smooth, seamless sides; and dropped-stitch ladders to let garments breathe and to allow fabrics worn beneath to peek though. Take inspiration from the styling shown in these photos, but remember that you can easily work these knits into your own wardrobe, whether life has you striding city avenues, circling suburbs, or settling in the country. Look for tips in the photo captions to help you pair the knits shown with garments already in your closet.

A few words about sizes: Over the years, I've experimented a great deal with stitches, knitwear construction, and yarns—especially the chunky ones I love so much—to play with scale and create the silhouettes I want for garments. The Northern Cross Sweater (page 40) illustrates how a roomy, boxy profile with boyish details can make a chunky knit fashion forward. Many Twinkle knits, though, feature a snug, body-shaping fit that looks equally fresh in big yarns. In the Nimbus Sweater (page 44), princess seams form a shapely fitted torso that contrasts with the gentle folds of the funnel neck. In some cases, proper fit means that the dimensions of the finished piece may be smaller than your actual body measurements. Forget what you've learned about chunky knits and needing extra ease—the yarns and stitches have a surprising amount of give to them, and many projects transform once you put them on. These patterns were written so that you can use your bust measurement as a general guide to selecting the size to knit, but every body is different. Check your hip and waist measurements against the schematics and pattern headnotes, where I've noted some details on fit to help you pick the right size.

Also, big stitches and deep rows mean that chunky knit designs require some special techniques for shaping. Don't be surprised when, in the patterns, you see asymmetrical bind-offs on sleeves, for instance, or notice decreases on both the front and back sides of some pieces. I've created these patterns carefully to make sure that the pieces can be seamed elegantly for flattering, youthful silhouettes. Be sure to read the pattern instructions closely before starting a project so you'll anticipate these special steps and get a sense of the piece's construction. Some of the individual pattern headnotes also include my thoughts on how designs should fit best.

Refer to the primer on knitting techniques (page 56). There, you'll find help mastering the knitting stitches and basic methods needed for the projects in *Twinkle's Weekend Knits*. In addition, I've sprinkled some "Twinkle Knit Bits"— knitting advice useful for beginner and experienced knitters—among the patterns.

So have you chosen your first pattern yet? Friday night approaches, and you'll want to be ready! No knitting marathons are required, though; there's time enough for fresh-air fun and finished projects. Just find a comfy place to relax with needles and yarn, along with some friends to admire your new knits!

THROUGHOUT THIS BOOK, USE THE FOLLOWING GUIDE TO CORRELATE YOUR BUST MEASUREMENT TO SIZE: XS = 31"-33" (78.5CM-84CM); S = 34"-36" (86CM-91CM); M = 37"-39" (94CM-99CM); L = 40"-42" (102CM-107CM). KNOW, TOO, THAT WHEN CALCULATING FINISHED GARMENT DIMENSIONS FROM GAUGE MEASUREMENTS, WE ROUNDED UP OR DOWN AS NEEDED TO MAKE THE RANGE BETWEEN SIZES UNIFORM. THUS, IT ISN'T A PROBLEM IF YOUR FINISHED MEASUREMENT IS OFF BY A HALF-INCH; THE PATTERNS AND YARNS ARE FORGIVING

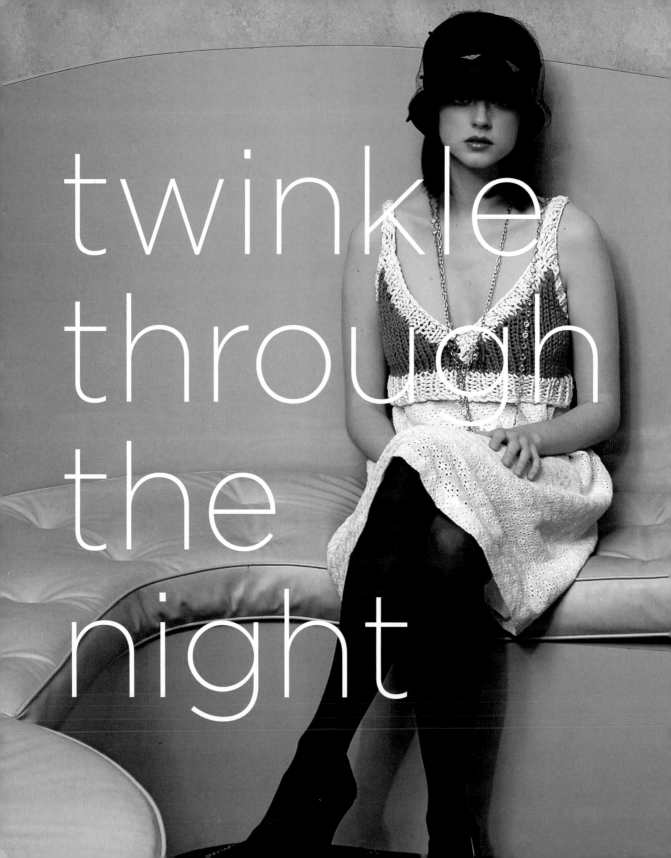

twinkle through the night

FRIDAY NIGHT

A getaway bag slung on your shoulder and a coat on your arm—it's your weekend escape. The trail of red taillights before you recedes, replaced by the pulsing glow of embers in a fireplace. The endless chirp of telephones melts into the call of crickets and the sound of fall leaves scuttling across porches. It's time to clear your mind and give your thoughts some space to flow. Perhaps there's light enough for an evening stroll before gathering friends for an elegant evening out.

For dressy events, these knits add depth and complexity to casual clothes; they work the Twinkle alchemy to transform yarn into something fresh, fashionable, and one-of-a-kind. Be daring when dressing for evenings out. Remember that the magic is in the mix. Side by side, patterns come together with beautiful results; unexpected colors coordinate in ways you never imagined. Contrasting textures—wool knits on silk, or silk yarns over suede—show off each other's best assets in sophisticated ways. And isn't that just the thing for the first night of your Twinkle getaway?

In this chapter, I'll introduce the bramble stitch, which is the basis for the sumptuous Lilac Mist Throw (page 28). You'll also learn to make a fabulous bobbled scarf and, working on straight and circular needles, some handy techniques for right-slanting decreases (k2tog), left-slanting ones (ssk), and increases.

boysenberry scarf

The Boysenberry Scarf's dramatic knotted fringe delivers a serious dose of glamour for the little work involved. Drape it over any outfit, even a chestnut-colored leather bomber jacket worn with vintage-wash or dark denim jeans.

page 68

wisteria scarf

Worn hanging down, this scarf cascades in neat vertical clusters of stitches, like wisteria blossoms. If you spread it out over your shoulders, you reveal its lacy open lattices. You can also loop it around your neck to add texture to a boxy toggle coat topping a pleated miniskirt, tights, and a platform loafer.

page 70

horizon

Live *la vie en rose* in this crisp yet feminine top, shown here in a classic color combination, or wear it to work over a pencil skirt with pointy patent pumps or a more traditionally styled pair. This knit has a surprisingly comfy (and sexy!) clinginess that comes from the springy silk-and-cotton yarn. The fitted torso permits a flattering and simply detailed scooped neckline.

page 72

tunic

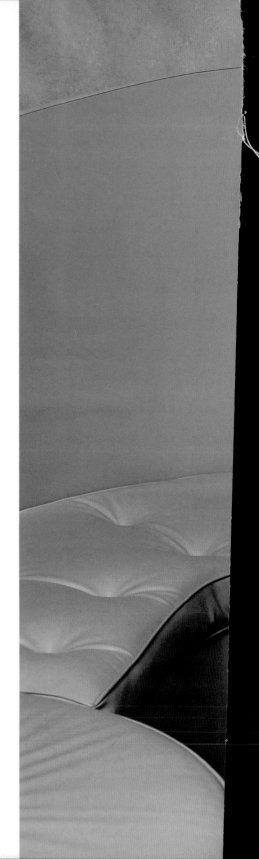

nightfall cropped top

Fashioned from lustrous silk-and-cotton yarn in hushed tones, this short top can stand alone with a skirt or pants, accessorize a dress worn beneath, or peek out from under a jacket or shawl. Consider pairing it with high-waisted, full-leg trousers and a chunky, low-heeled pump.

page 75

The Lilac Mist Throw's textured pattern is rendered beautifully in a fine-gauge mohair-blend yarn. It's nearly weightless as well as timeless. You may begin this pattern as a gift and discover that it has a perfect spot in your own wardrobe.

page 78

lilac mist
throw

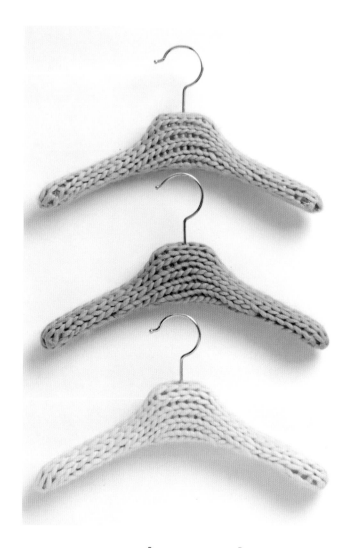

sand dune
hanger covers

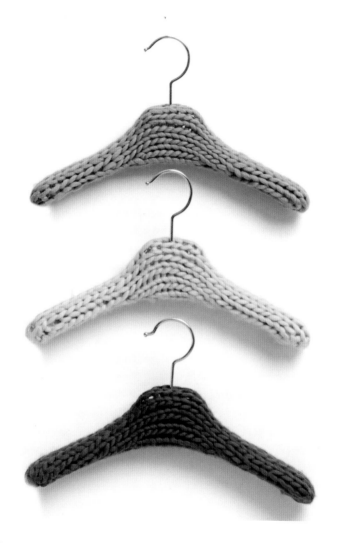

Looking for the perfect gift for the friend who has hosted your Twinkle weekend getaway? Or a hanger to keep that silk spaghetti-strap dress from landing in a puddle on the floor? Search no more. A trio of these hanger covers can be knit in no time and requires only a skein of Twinkle Handknits Soft Chunky wool.

page 80

fun alfresco

SATURDAY MORNING

Dawn rises like a curtain, sending light creeping around the edges of curtains and doors. Does your Saturday start with a jog around the lake, a Pilates video, or a bike ride to the farm stand? Or does the first morning of your getaway weekend commence, well, with an afternoon cup of coffee? No alarm clocks jolt you into consciousness; instead, songbirds coax you into the day. Legs stir first in the sheltered dark, like little tendrils of roots steadying the plant for sunshine and fresh air. Then you burst forth, radiant with color and cheer! There's nothing better than waking to a day destined for adventure and fun. No piles of mail to rifle through, no dry cleaning to fetch, no tresses to wheedle into obedient waves (you can always tame errant locks with the hats in this chapter).

Saturday's upbeat mood sets the tone for the pretty colors of this chapter's sporty patterns. With the exception of the iPod covers, these patterns call for chunky yarns. For tools, have on hand circular needles, straight needles, and double-pointed needles. You'll use seed stitch, among others, and I'll teach you a technique to make petal-like loops for the Peony Scarf (page 34).

snowcap hat
and peony scarf

Cuff this bold hat to top a white après-ski look: a parka, snow overalls, and pale furry boots. (Remember that a white and cream color scheme is pure Scandinavian chic!) Or pair it with a Mexican poncho, leather pants, and ankle boots. The Peony Scarf softens an Aran sweater and flannel trousers worn with spectator pumps in neutral tones.

snowcap hat, page 84; peony scarf, page 86

borealis sweater

Colors and patterns contrast
and harmonize amicably on the
funnel-necked Borealis Sweater.
Here, dashes accenting the
borders between colors echo
the dice-shaped dots in the skirt,
illustrating the Twinkle "pattern-
on-pattern" and "texture-on-
texture" styling to great effect.
The sweater's simple geometric
shape calls just as readily,
though, for trousers with
detailing and movement.
Pair this pullover with sailor
pants or other high-waisted
slacks worn with flat boots.

page 88

tidepool &
oceania sweaters,
equator iPod
sleeves

What to pack for your getaway to the Riviera? These vintage-inspired pullovers are *très belle, très chic* for seafaring and landlubbing weekenders alike. Nautical-themed details, such as the stripes and tie at the neck of the Tidepool Sweater and the flirty lace-tie front on the Oceania Sweater, are just as flattering and *charmant* when rendered in chunky yarns as in knitting worsted. For sportif outings, try the Tidepool with white capri pants and slides, and the Oceania with denim cutoffs and woven leather huaraches. Sailing choppy waters? Cushion your iPod and protect it from scratches with these two-tone covers.

tidepool sweater, page 91; oceania sweater, page 94; equator ipod sleeves, page 98

northern cross sweater and urchin beret

The playful shirttail hem and rolled edges on this sweater capture the casual, youthful spirit of Twinkle knits. Play off the Northern Cross's loose-fitted silhouette with white shorts and flat lace-up sandals. Wear the Urchin Beret with a luxurious off-white cashmere peacoat, black jeans, and flat-heeled boots in a textured skin.

40 *northern cross sweater, page 100;*
urchin beret, page 104

last
night
away

SUNDAY AFTERNOON

You've stowed your bicycle, closed up the boat, and perhaps uncorked some special wine. As dusk fades the lengthening shadows, a few evening stars appear in the sky. It's nearly time to return home. The change of scenery, as well as the slowed pace and rhythm, have gone a long way toward restoring your equilibrium. Pour yourself a glass of wine or make a pot of tea, because in the time it takes to finish either you can get a good start on the knit patterns in this chapter!

The palette for Sunday's knitting is serene and tranquil to reflect the mood of your last moments on holiday. This chapter's patterns require circular needles, straight needles, and a cable needle. You'll learn a pattern of stitches I call feather and fan stripes, to create an undulating stripe motif that you can adapt to your own creations, as well as the knot ridge stitch, which adds a quirky bump detail. I'll also introduce a wrapped-yarn increase and the dropped-stitch ladder that I love to use to create open, lacy sections in garments.

nimbus sweater

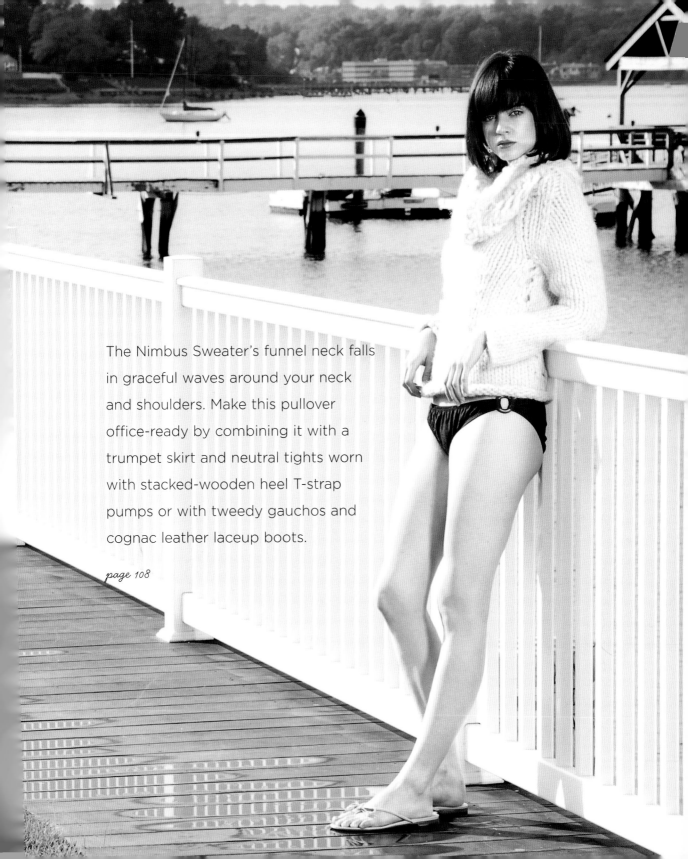

The Nimbus Sweater's funnel neck falls in graceful waves around your neck and shoulders. Make this pullover office-ready by combining it with a trumpet skirt and neutral tights worn with stacked-wooden heel T-strap pumps or with tweedy gauchos and cognac leather laceup boots.

page 108

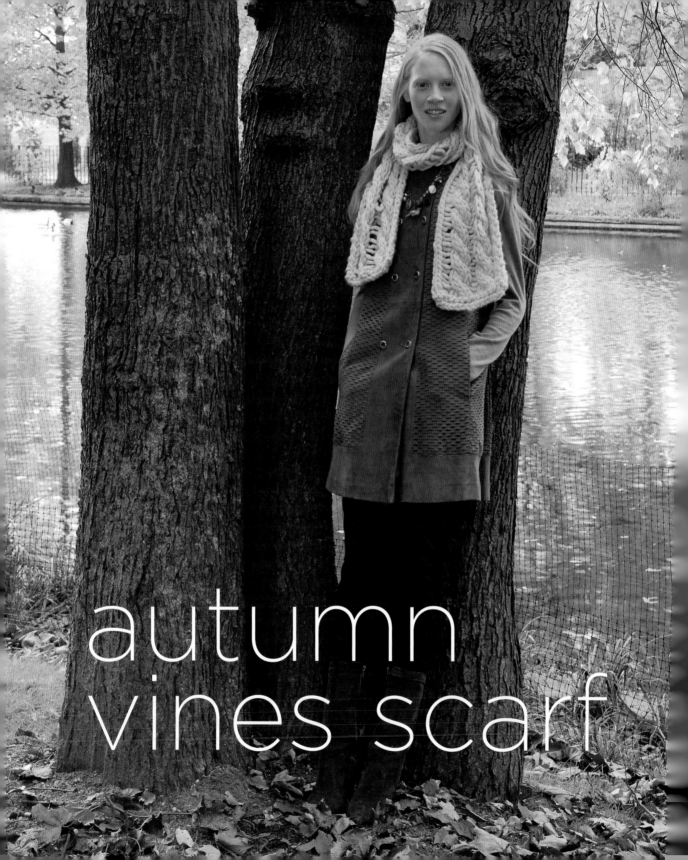

autumn
vines scarf

The delicate, lacy open sections allow a bit of skin to peek through, making this accessory both classic and sexy. Create a chic, arresting combination by pairing this updated cable scarf with a chiffon cocktail dress and lacy tights. Slip on high-heeled pumps to glam up the look. Autumn Vines knits up in a jiffy, so you can make several in different colors to keep or give as gifts!

page 112

riverbed
shawl

Stripes accentuate the undulating curves of this flirty shawl. Let them enhance yours! Pairing the black yarn with other yarns in pale, romantic colors—lavender or cream, for example—also creates a striking contrast. Perforations let a little bit of the garment worn underneath show through, and long fringe adds drama and movement. It's aristocratic, but in a modern, feminine way. You can wear it over a denim jacket with a suede miniskirt, wool tights, and flats or pair it with suede pants and ankle boots.

page 114

arbor row scarf

Loop the Arbor Row Scarf casually around your neck and let its vertical stripes lengthen your silhouette. A traditional pattern and colors are made fresh by the knit's exaggerated length and lively end panels running perpendicular to the body of the scarf. (You might try other cheery yarn colors against the white, too—orange and raspberry or red and brown would be charming choices.) Wear it as shown here, in a classic Twinkle collage of a delicate fabric and a chunky knit, or throw it over a fitted turtleneck so it grazes the well-worn knees of your favorite jeans tucked into knee-high, lace-up moccasins.

page 116

cloudburst
cardigan

This versatile cardi could become your favorite knit. Slip it on over your best cords, a comfy long-sleeved tee, and cowboy boots for a stroll to the farm stand, or layer it over a filmy dress or skirt for a nightcap at the local inn. Seamless sides, sleek contouring, and an attached edge piece that dissolves into a ruffle coalesce as an elegant, sophisticated knit that you can dress up or down.

page 118

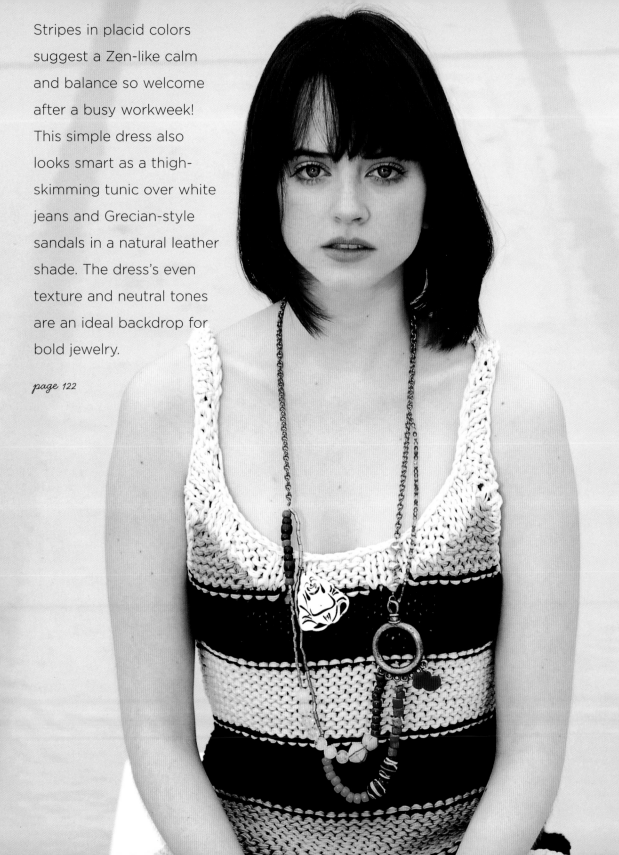

Stripes in placid colors suggest a Zen-like calm and balance so welcome after a busy workweek! This simple dress also looks smart as a thigh-skimming tunic over white jeans and Grecian-style sandals in a natural leather shade. The dress's even texture and neutral tones are an ideal backdrop for bold jewelry.

page 122

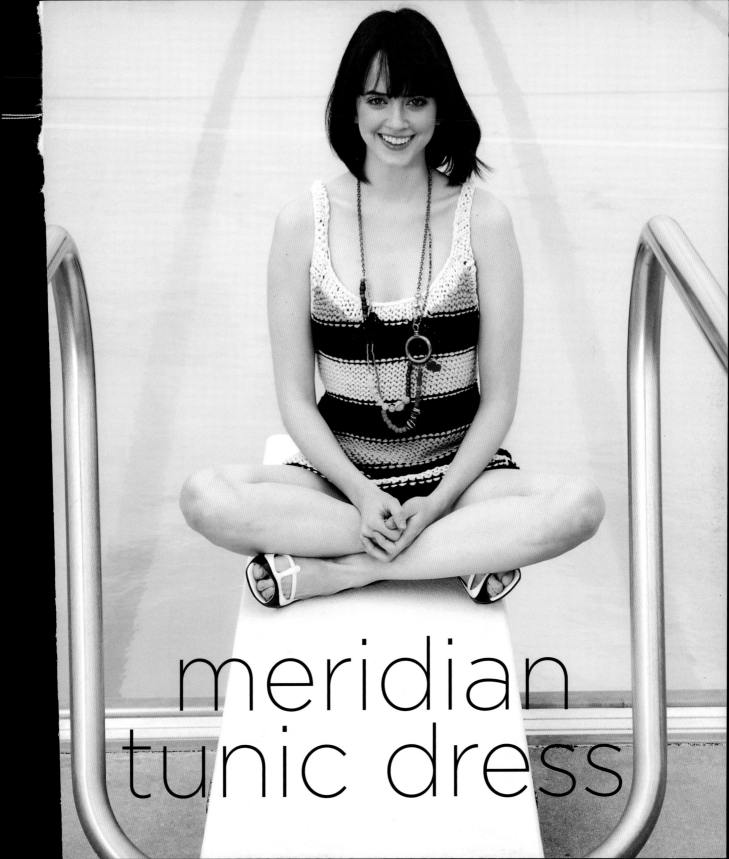

meridian
tunic dress

twinkle
tips

PREPARING FOR
A PROJECT

First, take the time to build up your confidence and basic skills. Start every design by reviewing its schematic, chart, and stitch pattern. Learn new approaches and hone your skills by experimenting with stitches on a small swatch. Many of my friends start projects, put them down, and never finish them because they become too frustrated. Don't worry about mistakes; you can easily correct them, and they become part of the learning curve, another step on your road to success as a knitter.

With proper preparation, you will be ready to knit any of these Twinkle patterns!

When you complete a project and the design comes to life, you'll be showered with compliments and inspired to knit up something else.

KNITTING IN
THE ROUND

We love going in circles! Knitting with short circular needles is modern and convenient. Circular needles fit into any hip handbag and travel everywhere. Since you don't need to join seams, you can knit all the way through without stopping.

Circular needles, available in many lengths, should be short enough to hold all your stitches without stretching them. I often use two circular needles to work on small necklines when the shortest circular needle is still too long. To accomplish this, divide the stitches evenly between two circular needles and knit with one circular needle at a time.

Although most patterns you'll find elsewhere are written for straight single-pointed needles, you can easily adjust the pattern for circular knitting. Here's some Twinkle Tips for adapting a flat pattern to a circular knit design:

- The right side is always facing you.
- When working on multiple stitch patterns, take out the stitches that are outside the repeat.
- Reverse wrong-side rows by reading the chart from right to left and making opposite stitches (for example, knit purl stitches and purl knit stitches).

CHILL WITH A CHUNKY

Often, I design sweaters just because I fall in love with a particular yarn. It could be anything about the yarn—texture, color, or even the challenge of not knowing how to design with it. When I first learned to knit, I enjoyed working with chunky yarn because it is fast. Now, I have grown to appreciate its many facets and capabilities.

Yarns have personality. The bulkier and softer the yarn, the more difficult it is to achieve consistency in gauge. Its inconsistencies add an artistic element to the design. Bulky yarn inherently appears stiffer. Through knitting, I work the flaws of chunky yarn to its advantage. For quirky, tiny sweaters, I like to exaggerate the bulk and pile it up, making cables, bobbles, or anything three-dimensional. Conversely, with lacy, open-weave patterns, I love creating intricate sheer effects that are perfect for lingerie or deconstructed looks.

Be adventurous with chunkies! Remake a pattern you like in rainbow stripes instead of solids. Revitalize an old design by using a heavier yarn and a larger needle. You will discover the joy of creating something unexpected from the familiar.

GO FOR IT WITH GAUGE

Gauge determines your design's measurements. Before knitting a sweater, make a swatch to ensure that you can achieve the correct gauge. If most of the garment is to be made in a pattern stitch, make a swatch in that pattern stitch.

For chunkies, the stitch gauge is fewer than three stitches to an inch (2.5cm), so exact gauge is crucial. For accuracy, I suggest making a larger swatch and measuring from the middle. Make it match: If your gauge does not match the example precisely, use a larger or smaller needle until it's right.

Some knitters notice that when knitting in the round, their tension is tighter. You might find that your gauge is different from the swatch knit flat on straight needles. Work on a gauge swatch in the round to know for sure.

KNITTING TECHNIQUES

Stockinette Stitch

Knit right-side rows;
purl wrong-side rows.

Stockinette Stitch in the Round

Knit all rounds.

Reverse Stockinette Stitch

Purl right-side rows;
knit wrong-side rows.

Reverse Stockinette Stitch in the Round

Purl all rounds.

Garter Stitch

Knit all rows.

Garter Stitch in the Round

Rnd 1: Knit.
Rnd 2: Purl.

Seed Stitch

ROW/RND 1: ★K1, p1; rep from ★.
ROW/RND 2: Purl the knit sts and knit the purl sts.
Rep Row/Rnd 2 for pattern.

K1, P1 Rib

ROW/RND 1: ★K1, p1; rep from ★.
ROW/RND 2: Knit the knit sts and purl the purl sts.
Rep Row/Rnd 2 for pattern.

K2, P2 Rib

ROW/RND 1: ★K2, p2; rep from ★.
ROW/RND 2: Knit the knit sts and purl the purl sts.
Rep Row/Rnd 2 for pattern.

Attaching Fringe

Holding two or more strands together, fold strands in half. Insert crochet hook from back to front of garment edge and pull doubled strands through. Draw yarn ends through loop and pull tight (see illus.).

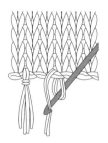

Increases and Decreases

Most increases and decreases should be fully fashioned. In other words, whenever possible they should be made one stitch away from the edge of the fabric, or from the stitch markers, according to the pattern.

Joining Stitches

- On circular needles (illus. 1).
- On double-pointed needles (illus. 2).
- Make sure stitches are not twisted when you're joining.

Making Buttonholes

- When you make a buttonhole with chunky yarn, binding off one stitch may be sufficient.
- For lighter-weight yarn, bind off more stitches, based on the button size (illus. 1).
- On next row, use the e-loop method to cast on the same number of stitches that were bound off on the previous row (illus. 2).

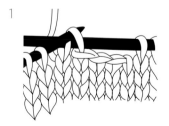

Markers

- Using markers is extremely important when you're knitting in the round (illus. 1 and 2).
- Used on the sides, center, front, and back, markers enable you to keep track of the beginning and the end.

Picking Up Stitches

- On vertical edges, pick up one stitch in between each row (illus. 1 and 2).
- On horizontal edges, pick up one stitch in between each stitch (illus. 3 and 4).
- On slanted edges, pick up using the vertical or horizontal techniques described above (illus. 5).

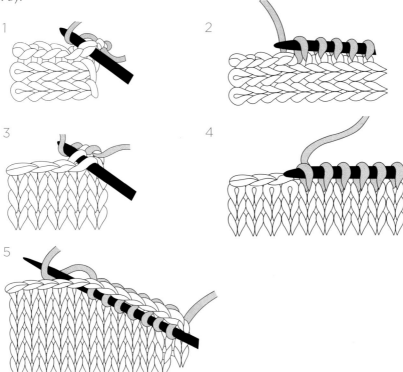

Seaming/Sewing

To seam finished pieces in stockinette stitch or reverse stockinette stitch together, select from the techniques outlined below.

- To get started (illus. 1), insert needle from the back (WS) to the front (RS) in the corner stitches of each piece you want to sew together. Pull tightly to close the gap.

- For vertical seams on stockinette stitch (illus. 2), use mattress stitch: Insert needle under the horizontal bar created by the edge stitch and the stitch next to it. Pull the yarn through and insert the needle into the corresponding bar on the opposite piece. Continue to work back and forth.

- For vertical seams on reverse stockinette stitch (illus. 3), insert needle into the loop created by the edge stitch. Pull the yarn through and insert the needle into the bottom loop of the corresponding stitch on the opposite piece. Continue to work back and forth.

- For horizontal seams in stockinette stitch (illus. 4), insert needle under a stitch inside the bound-off edge of one side. Pull yarn through and insert the needle under the corresponding stitch on the opposite side.

- For vertical-to-horizontal seams (illus. 5), insert needle under a stitch inside the bound-off edge of the horizontal piece. Pull through and insert needle under the horizontal bar between the first and second stitch of the vertical piece.

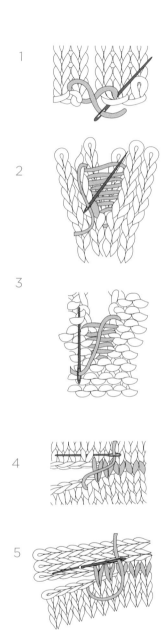

1

2

3

4

5

Short Rows

Short rows are made by working part of the way across a row, then turning and working back. However, in order to avoid a hole, you must "wrap" each stitch at the turning point. To wrap a stitch when the last stitch worked is a knit stitch: Knit to the turning point, slip next stitch onto right-hand needle purlwise (illus.1), bring yarn between needles (illus.2), slip stitch onto left-hand needle (illus.3), turn. Work in a similar manner when on the purl side (illus.4–6).

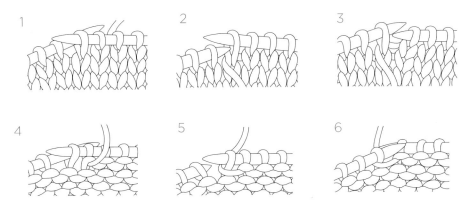

Three-Needle Bind-Off

Hold pieces to be joined with wrong sides together, needles parallel to each other and pointing to the right.

1. Insert right-hand needle into the first stitch on the front needle and into the first stitch on the back needle, and knit these two stitches together. One stitch is now on the right-hand needle.
2. Knit together the next pair of stitches in the same way.
3. Slip the first stitch on the right needle over the second stitch to bind it off.
4. Repeat the last two steps until one stitch remains on needle. Fasten off.

Using Stitch Holders

Try using waste yarn as a holder to keep from squeezing many stitches onto a small stitch holder.

ABBREVIATIONS

Ch chain

K knit

K2tog knit 2 together

M1 make 1 increase—On the knit side: Insert tip of right hand needle from front to back into the strand running between the two needles, lift this strand onto the left-hand needle, insert the right-hand needle into the stitch knitwise, knit this stitch. On the purl side: Insert the tip of the right-hand needle from front to back into the strand running between the two needles, lift this strand onto the left-hand needle, insert the right-hand needle into the stitch purlwise, and purl this stitch.

P purl

P2tog purl 2 sts together—creates a right-leaning decrease on the purl side of the fabric

Rnd round

RS right side

Ssk slip, slip, knit—Slip next 2 sts one at a time as if to knit, insert the left-hand needle into both stitches as if to knit, and knit those stitches together—creates a left-leaning decrease on the knit side of the fabric.

Ssp slip, slip, purl—Slip next 2 stitches one at a time as if to knit to the right-hand needle, pass them back together to the left-hand needle, and purl those two stitches together through back loop (tbl)—creates a left-leaning decrease on the knit side of the fabric.

Sts stitches

WS wrong side

yo yarn over—Bring the yarn over the needle.

friday
night:
twinkle
through
the night

This chic scarf is a snap to knit once you've mastered the bobble technique. The whimsical raised bobbles stand out against their stockinette background. The double-knotted fringe gives this accessory an artist-aristocrat vibe. You can follow the text instructions, or refer to the stitch chart if you prefer.

boysenberry scarf

PAGE 20

SIZE
One Size

KNITTED MEASUREMENTS
11" x 42" (28cm x 106.5cm) excluding fringe

MATERIALS

 super bulky

2 hanks Twinkle Handknits Soft Chunky, 100% virgin merino wool, 7 oz/200g, 83 yds/75m, #02 Raspberry

US size 19 (15mm) needles or size needed to obtain gauge

Tapestry needle

Large crochet hook (size P/Q [15mm]) for attaching fringe

GAUGE
13 stitches = 7" (18cm) and 15 rows = 7" (18cm) in garter stitch (see page 59) after blocking

TAKE THE TIME TO CHECK YOUR GAUGE.

ABBREVIATION
MB (make bobble)—(K1, p1, k1) into next stitch, turn, p3, turn, k3, turn, p3, turn, sl 1, k2tog, pass slipped stitch over.

TWINKLE KNIT BIT
REMEMBER THAT WHEN LOOKING AT PATTERNS SET IN GRID DIAGRAMS, THE ODD-NUMBERED ROWS ARE READ—IN TERMS OF THE ORDER OF THE STITCHES—FROM RIGHT TO LEFT, AND THE EVEN-NUMBERED ROWS ARE READ FROM LEFT TO RIGHT.

SCARF

Cast on 17 stitches.

ROW 1 (RS): Knit.

ROWS 2, 4, 6, AND 8: Purl.

ROWS 3 AND 7: K5, ★MB, k5; repeat from ★ across.

ROW 5: K2, ★MB, k5; repeat from ★ once, MB, k2.

ROWS 9-12: Purl.

ROWS 13-16: Repeat rows 5–8.

ROWS 17-76: Knit.

ROW 77 (RS): Knit.

ROWS 78, 80, AND 82: Purl.

ROW 79: Repeat row 3.

ROW 81: Repeat row 5.

ROWS 83-86: Purl.

ROWS 87-92: Repeat rows 3–8.

ROW 93: Knit.

Bind off. Weave in ends.

TRIPLE-KNOTTED FRINGE

Cut 36 lengths of yarn 34" (86.5cm) long. Attach 9 sets of double-stranded fringe evenly spaced along each end of the Scarf. For the second set of knots, using an overhand knot, tie together half the strands from one fringe with half from the adjacent fringe, making knots about 1" (2.5cm) down from the first set of knots. Make a third row of knots using half of the strands from each knotted group. Trim the ends.

FINISHING

Steam block the center garter stitch portion to set the Scarf length.

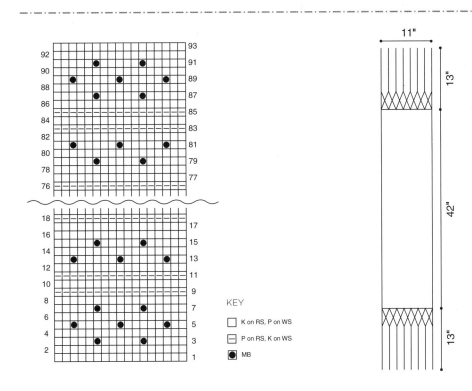

KEY

☐ K on RS, P on WS

⊟ P on RS, K on WS

◉ MB

wisteria scarf PAGE 22

SIZE
One Size

KNITTED MEASUREMENTS
13½" x 49" (33cm x 124.5cm) excluding fringe

MATERIALS

 super bulky

2 hanks Twinkle Handknits Soft Chunky, 100% virgin merino wool, 7 oz/200g, 83 yds/75m, #26 Lilac

US size 36 (20mm) needles or size needed to obtain gauge

Tapestry needle

Large crochet hook (size P/Q [15mm]) for attaching fringe

GAUGE
15 stitches = 13" (33cm) in openwork rib pattern

TAKE THE TIME TO CHECK YOUR GAUGE.

The Wisteria Scarf's lattice pattern results from the series of yarn over increases and the "slip, slip, knit" (ssk) and "purl 2 together" (p2tog) decreases worked on oversize needles. The extra-long fringe adds movement and interest; a sharp pair of sewing scissors will help you trim it evenly. You can easily adjust this scarf's length to suit your height.

OPENWORK RIB PATTERN (MULTIPLE OF 4)

ROW 1 (RS): ★K2, yo, ssk; repeat from ★.
ROW 2: ★P2, yo, p2tog; repeat from ★.
Repeat rows 1 and 2 for pattern.

SCARF

Cast on 16 stitches. Work Openwork Rib Pattern until the piece measures approximately 49" (124.5cm). Bind off loosely. Weave in ends.

FRINGE

Cut 48 lengths of yarn 26" (66cm) long. Attach 12 sets of double-stranded fringe evenly across each end of the Scarf (page 60). Trim the ends.

TWINKLE KNIT BIT

SOONER OR LATER, ESPECIALLY WHEN WORKING WITH BIG NEEDLES, YOU'RE GOING TO HAVE WORK FALL OFF YOUR NEEDLES. PUTTING THE STITCHES BACK ON YOUR NEEDLE CAN BE PERPLEXING. REMEMBER THAT A PROPERLY SITUATED STITCH RESTS SO THAT THE FRONT OF THE LOOP—THE SIDE CLOSEST TO YOUR BODY WHEN HOLDING YOUR KNITTING—IS PULLED SLIGHTLY TO THE RIGHT (ON YOUR LEFT NEEDLE, TOWARD THE POINTED TIP). THE PART OF THE LOOP TO THE REAR OF THE NEEDLE LEANS LEFTWARD. KEEPING A POINT PROTECTOR OR A RUBBER BAND WRAPPED AROUND THE END OF A NEEDLE WILL HELP PREVENT MISHAPS WHEN YOU'RE NOT WORKING ON THE PIECE.

KEY

	K on RS, P on WS
	yo
	P2tog on WS
	SSK on RS

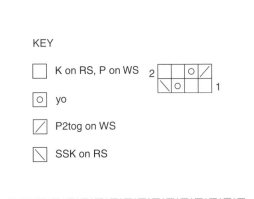

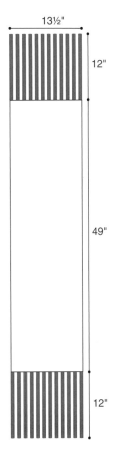

Holding four strands together as you knit creates a subtly textured fabric with give and stretch. This elasticity yields snug bust and torso dimensions that hold the shoulders in place and allow for the dramatic neckline. (Don't be concerned that your bust measures a good bit larger than the knit garment—the negative ease is needed for a good fit.) The neckline features a charming detail—a narrow cabled band that is attached later.

horizon tunic PAGE 24

SIZE
XS (S, M, L)

REMEMBER TO USE THIS GUIDE TO FIND YOUR SIZE BASED ON YOUR ACTUAL BUST MEASUREMENT: XS = 31"–33" (79cm–84cm); S = 34"–36" (86cm–91cm); M = 37"–39" (94cm–99cm); L = 40"–42" (102cm–107cm).

KNITTED MEASUREMENTS
Bust: 26 (27½, 29, 30½)" (66 [70, 74, 77.5]cm)

Back length: 27 (28, 28, 30)" (68.5 [71, 71, 76]cm)

MATERIALS
 fine

8 (8, 9, 10) balls Twinkle Handknits Cruise, 70% silk/30% cotton, 1³/₄ oz/50g, 120 yds/109m, #09 Black (A)

3 (3, 4, 4) balls #08 White (B)

US size 15 (10mm) 24" (60cm) circular needle or size needed to obtain gauge

Stitch holder

Stitch markers

Tapestry needle

GAUGE
10 stitches and 12 rows = 4" (10cm) in stockinette stitch (see page 59) with 4 strands held together

TAKE THE TIME TO CHECK YOUR GAUGE.

NOTES
The Sleeves are first knit flat, then the Body is knit in the round. The Sleeves and Neck Band are worked back and forth on the circular needle. The Sleeves are joined to the Body at the underarm, and the sweater is knit in one piece from that point. The stitch marker at the beginning of the round should be a different color from the others. The entire piece is worked in stockinette stitch with 4 strands of yarn held together, then turned inside out to use the "wrong" side as the right side. Weave in ends on the knit side of the fabric.

ABBREVIATIONS
Inc 1—Knit 1 in the row below the next stitch, knit the next stitch.
C4L (cable 4 left)—Slip the next 2 stitches to a cable needle and hold in front of the work, k2, k2 from the cable needle.

CABLE PATTERN (8 STITCHES) See page 74.

ROWS 1 AND 5 (RS): P2, k4, p2.

ROWS 2 AND 4: K2, p4, k2.

ROW 3: P2, C4L, p2.

ROW 6: K2, p4, k2.

Repeat rows 1–6 for pattern.

SLEEVES (MAKE 2)

With 4 strands of A held together, long-tail cast on 20 (22, 24, 26) stitches. Knit 1 row. Change to stockinette stitch and inc 1 each edge every 6th row 4 times—28 (30, 32, 34) stitches. Work even until the sleeve measures approximately 8 (8, 8, 9)" (20.5 [20.5, 20.5, 23]cm). Bind off 1 stitch at the beginning of the next 2 rows—26 (28, 30, 32) stitches. Place the remaining stitches on a holder.

BODY

With 4 strands of B held together, cast on 16 (17, 18, 19) stitches, place marker to indicate the underarm, cast on 32 (34, 36, 38) stitches, place marker to indicate the underarm, cast on 16 (17, 18, 19) stitches, place marker to indicate the center front and the beginning of the round—64 (68, 72, 76) stitches. Join, being careful not to twist stitches. Purl 1 round. Change to stockinette stitch and work even until the piece measures 9" (23cm) from the beginning. Change to A and work 11 rounds even.

NEXT RND (DECREASE RND): Knit to 2 stitches before the first underarm marker, ssk, slip marker, k2tog, knit to 2 stitches before the second underarm marker, ssk, slip marker, k2tog, knit to end of round—60 (64, 68, 72) stitches.

Work 5 rounds even; repeat Decrease Rnd—56 (60, 64, 68) stitches. Work 12 rounds even.

NEXT RND (INCREASE RND): Knit to 2 stitches before the first underarm marker, inc 1, k1, slip marker, k1, inc 1, knit to 2 stitches before the second underarm marker, inc 1, k1, slip marker, k1, inc 1, knit to end of round—60 (64, 68, 72) stitches.

SIZES XS AND S ONLY: Work 5 rounds even; repeat Increase Rnd, ending 2 stitches before the beginning-of-round marker—64 (68) stitches.

SIZES M AND L ONLY: Work 5 rounds even; repeat Increase Round. Work 2 (4) rounds even, ending 2 stitches before the beginning-of-round marker—72 (76) stitches.

FRONT NECK AND ARMHOLE SHAPING

NOTE: READ ALL SHAPING INSTRUCTIONS BEFORE BEGINNING.

Removing the marker, bind off 4 stitches, knit to end of round, turn—60 (64, 68, 72) stitches. Work 3 rows even in stockinette stitch.

NEXT ROW: Removing the markers, ssk, ★knit to 2 stitches before the underarm marker, bind off 4 stitches; repeat from ★ once, knit to the last 2 stitches, k2tog, turn—11 (12, 13, 14) left front stitches, 28 (30, 32, 34) back stitches, 11 (12, 13, 14) right front stitches.

JOIN THE SLEEVES AND BODY

Work to the armhole edge, place marker for the raglan shaping, work 26 (28, 30, 32) Sleeve stitches, place marker for the raglan shaping, work 28 (30, 32, 34) back stitches, place marker for the raglan shaping, work 26 (28, 30, 32) Sleeve stitches, place marker for the raglan shaping, work to end—102 (110, 118, 126) stitches.

Continue to decrease 1 stitch at each front neck edge every fourth row 3 (3, 2, 1) more time(s), then every other row 0 (0, 2, 4) time(s), and *at the same time*, work 2 more rows in stockinette stitch, then work the raglan shaping on the next and every knit row a total of 6 (7, 7, 7) times as follows: ★Work to 3 stitches before the marker, k2tog, k1, slip marker, k1, ssk; repeat from ★ 3 times, then work to end of row—16 (16, 18, 20) back stitches, 12 (12, 14, 14) Sleeve stitches, and 2 front stitches on each side remain when all shaping is complete. Bind off.

NECK BAND

With 4 strands of A held together, provisional cast on 8 stitches. Work in cable pattern for 124 (124, 130, 130) rows—20 (20, 21, 21) cable turns are complete. Place cast-on stitches on one end of the circular needle. With right sides together and using the second straight needle, work a three-needle bind-off (page 63) across all stitches.

FINISHING

Turn the sweater inside out so that the purl side becomes the right side. With the right side facing and using mattress stitch (page 62), sew the Sleeve and underarm seams. Sew the Neck Band around the neck edge, placing the seam at the center back. Weave in ends on the wrong side.

KEY

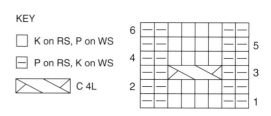

□ K on RS, P on WS

⊟ P on RS, K on WS

⊠ C 4L

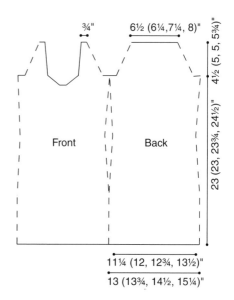

¾"

6½ (6¼, 7¼, 8)"

4½ (5, 5, 5¾)"

23 (23, 23¾, 24¼)"

Front   Back

11¼ (12, 12¾, 13½)"

13 (13¾, 14½, 15¼)"

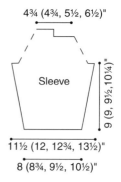

4¾ (4¾, 5½, 6½)"

Sleeve

9 (9, 9½, 10¼)"

11½ (12, 12¾, 13½)"

8 (8¾, 9½, 10½)"

After working most of this garment in stockinette, you'll pick up stitches along the edges of the armholes and neckline and knit a narrow rib for good fit. This pattern relies on some traditional shaping methods for increases and decreases. You can either knit 2 together (k2tog) for a right-slanting decrease, or do a "slip, slip, knit" (ssk) sequence for a left-slanting one.

nightfall cropped top

PAGE 26

SIZE
XS (S, M, L)

REMEMBER TO USE THIS GUIDE TO FIND YOUR SIZE BASED ON YOUR ACTUAL BUST MEASUREMENT: XS = 31″–33″ (79cm–84cm); S = 34″–36″ (86cm–91cm); M = 37″–39″ (94cm–99cm); L = 40″–42″ (102cm–107cm). Here, your actual measurement may measure 10″ (25cm) larger than the knitted measurements, and you're still good to go. The negative ease allows for a flattering fit and is possible due to the yarn's stretchiness.

KNITTED MEASUREMENTS
Bust: 24 (25½, 27, 28½)″ (61 [65, 68.5, 72]cm)

MATERIALS

 fine

3 balls Twinkle Handknits Cruise, 70% silk/30% cotton, 1¾ oz/50g, 120 yds/109m, #08 White (A)

2 balls #64 Cobble Stone (B)

US size 13 (9mm) 24″ (60cm) circular needles
US size 15 (10mm) 24″ (60cm) circular needles or size needed to obtain gauge

Stitch markers

Stitch holder

Tapestry needle

GAUGE
10 stitches and 12 rows = 4″ (10cm) in stockinette stitch (see page 59) with 4 strands held together on size 15 (10mm) needles

TAKE THE TIME TO CHECK YOUR GAUGE.

ABBREVIATION
Inc 1—Knit 1 in the row below the next stitch, knit the next stitch.

NOTES
The top is begun in the round and then divided and knit back and forth on a circular needle. Four strands of yarn are held together throughout.

BODY

With the smaller circular needle and 4 strands of A held together, cast on 60 (64, 68, 72) stitches. Place marker to indicate the center front and the beginning of the round. Join, being careful not to twist stitches. Work 8 rounds in k1, p1 rib (page 59).

Change to 4 strands of B and the larger circular needle.

NEXT RND (INCREASE RND): K5 (6, 7, 8), inc 1, k1, inc 1, k7, place marker to indicate the right underarm, k7, inc 1, k1, inc 1, k10 (12, 14, 16), inc 1, k1, inc 1, k7, place marker to indicate the left underarm, k7, inc 1, k1, inc 1, knit to end of round—68 (72, 76, 80) stitches. Knit 1 round.

DIVIDE FOR THE FRONT NECK

ROW 1 (RS): Knit to end of round, turn.
ROW 2: Purl.
ROW 3 (RS DECREASE ROW): K2tog, knit to last 2 stitches, ssk—66 (70, 74, 78) stitches.
ROW 4: Purl.
ROW 5: Knit.
ROW 6 (WS DECREASE ROW): Ssp, purl to last 2 stitches, p2tog—64 (68, 72, 76) stitches.
ROWS 7–9: Repeat rows 1–3—62 (66, 70, 74) stitches.

DIVIDE FOR THE ARMHOLES

Removing the markers as you work, purl to 2 stitches before the first marker, join another ball of yarn, bind off 4 stitches, purl to 2 stitches before the next marker and place these 30 (32, 34, 36) stitches on a holder for the Back, bind off 4 stitches, purl to end of row—12 (13, 14, 15) stitches each side.

Working the left and right fronts with separate balls of yarn, continue to decrease 1 stitch at each neck edge every 3 rows 5 (5, 4, 5) more times, then every 0 (0, 4, 2) row(s) once, and *at the same time*, at the armhole edge work even 2 (1, 1, 1) row(s), then decrease 1 stitch each armhole edge the next row, then every other row 5 (6, 7, 7) more times. When all shaping is complete, 1 stitch remains. End off.

BACK

Place the Back stitches on the larger needle. Beginning with a right-side row, work 2 rows even.

DIVIDE FOR THE BACK NECK AND ARMHOLE SHAPING

Working armhole decreases as for the front, work until the Back measures 4½ (4½, 4¾, 5)" (10 [10, 12.5, 13]cm) from end of ribbing. Bind off the center 8 (8, 10, 12) stitches. Working both sides at once with separate balls of yarn and maintaining armhole decreases, decrease 1 stitch each neck edge every 2 (2, 3, 3) rows 4 (4, 3, 3) times—1 stitch remains when all shaping is complete. Bind off.

NECK BANDS

With the right side facing and using the smaller needle and 4 strands of A, pick up and knit 26 (26, 28, 30) stitches along the back neck. Work 3 rows in k1, p1 rib. Bind off in rib.

With the right side facing and using smaller needle and 4 strands of A, pick up and knit 23 (23, 24, 24) stitches along the left front neck to the center, place marker, pick up and knit 23 (23, 24, 24) stitches along right front neck—46 (46, 48, 48) stitches.

ROW 1 (WS): K1(1, 0, 0), *p1, k1; repeat from * to 2 stitches before the marker, ssp, slip marker, p2tog, *k1, p1; repeat from * to last 1 (1, 0, 0) stitch, p1 (1, 0, 0)—44 (44, 46, 46) stitches.

ROW 2: Work in established rib to 2 stitches before the marker, k2tog, slip marker, ssk, work in rib to end—42 (42, 44, 44) stitches.

ROW 3: Work in established rib to 2 stitches before the marker, ssp, slip marker, p2tog, work in rib to end—40 (40, 42, 42) stitches.
Bind off in rib.

LEFT ARM BAND

With the right side facing and using the smaller needle and 4 strands of A, beginning at the left underarm edge, pick up and knit 20 (21, 21, 21) stitches along the front armhole edge, cast on 16 (16, 18, 20) stitches, pick up and knit 20 (21, 21, 21) stitches along the back armhole edge, place marker to indicate the beginning of the round— 56 (58, 60, 62) stitches. Work 3 rounds in k1, p1 rib. Bind off in rib.

RIGHT ARM BAND

Make as for the Left Arm Band, picking up stitches along the back armhole edge first.

FINISHING

Weave in ends.

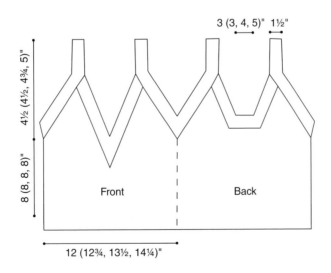

In the bramble stitch, you'll knit and purl three times into a single stitch and then gather together the next three stitches to create a textured field that is vintage in feel but rendered modern by being framed in dropped-stitch ladders. The openwork edges—in addition to the luxurious lightness of the yarn—yield a throw so delicate it seems to roll in like a fog.

lilac mist throw PAGE 28

SIZE
One Size

KNITTED MEASUREMENTS
48" x 72" (122cm x 183cm)

MATERIALS

 fine

9 balls Twinkle Handknits Kids Mohair, 40% wool/35% mohair/25% acrylic, 1¾ oz/50g, 310 yds/283m, #49 Silver Lavender

US size 15 (10mm) 29" (75cm) circular needle or size needed to obtain gauge

Stitch markers

Tapestry needle

GAUGE
16 stitches and 13 rows = 10" (25.5cm) in bramble stitch

TAKE THE TIME TO CHECK YOUR GAUGE.

NOTE
A circular needle is used to accommodate the large number of stitches; work back and forth in rows.

TWINKLE KNIT BIT

IF YOU CAN'T DETERMINE THE FIBER CONTENT OF THE YARN YOU'RE USING—FOR EXAMPLE, IF YOU LOSE THE SKEIN'S LABEL OR CAN'T OBTAIN THE YARN SPECIFIED IN THE PATTERN—YOU CAN BURN A LITTLE BIT OF IT TO IDENTIFY ITS CONTENT BY SMELL. EACH FIBER HAS A UNIQUE ODOR WHEN BURNED. HERE ARE SOME FIBERS AND WHAT THEY SMELL LIKE WHEN A LIGHTER IS TAKEN TO THEM:

ACRYLIC: MELTING PLASTIC

SILK: BURNING HAIR

WOOL: A SHEEP

COTTON: A BURNING CANDLEWICK

BAMBOO: A BARBECUE SKEWER FROM THE GRILL

BRAMBLE STITCH (MULTIPLE OF 4 + 2)

ROWS 1 AND 3 (RS): Purl.

ROW 2: K1, ★(k1, p1, k1) into the next stitch, p3tog; repeat from ★ to last stitch, k1.

ROW 4: K1, ★p3tog, (k1, p1, k1) into the next stitch; repeat from ★ to last stitch, k1.

Repeat rows 1–4 for pattern.

THROW

Cast on 138 stitches.

ROW 1 (RS): K3, place marker, k3, place marker, work row 1 of bramble stitch across the next 126 stitches, place marker, k3, place marker, k3.

ROW 2: P6, work in bramble stitch to the next marker, p6.

Continue in established pattern until the piece measures approximately 48" (122cm), ending with a wrong-side row.

NEXT ROW (BIND-OFF ROW): Bind off 2 stitches (1 stitch on the right-hand needle), remove marker, drop the next 3 stitches from the needle, remove marker, pull the loop on the right-hand needle to the correct length to reach across the gap made by the dropped stitches, bind off stitches to the next marker, remove marker, drop the next 3 stitches from the needle, remove marker, pull the loop on the right-hand needle across the gap, bind off remaining stitches.

Ladder the 3 dropped stitches on each side all the way down to the cast-on row.

Weave in all ends.

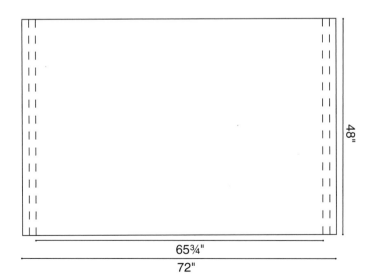

This delightful project requires little yarn and only a few increases and decreases. Knit up a rounded rectangle, and then feed the hanger's hook end between the stitches in the middle of the knit piece. Use the end tails of the yarn like drawstrings to shape the cast-on stitches and the end row to the hanger's contours. One seam at the bottom is all it takes to enclose the hanger.

sand dune hanger covers PAGE 30

SIZE
One Size

KNITTED MEASUREMENTS
To fit 15½" (39.5cm) long x 1½" (3.8cm) wide plastic coat hanger

MATERIALS

 super bulky

1 hank Twinkle Handknits Soft Chunky, 100% virgin merino wool, 7 oz/200g, 83 yds/75m, in any of the following: #26 Lilac, #18 French Grey, #25 Powder, #23 Haze, #20 Icy Blue, #27 Urchin

US size 19 (15mm) needles or size needed to obtain gauge

Tapestry needle

GAUGE
9 stitches and 9 rows = 5" (12.5cm) in stockinette stitch (see page 59)

TAKE THE TIME TO CHECK YOUR GAUGE.

NOTE
One skein makes 3 hanger covers.

COVER

Leaving a 12" (30.5cm) tail, cast on 9 stitches. Work 10 rows in stockinette stitch. Increase 1 stitch (using M1) at each edge on the next 2 right-side rows—13 stitches. Work 9 rows even. Knit 2 together at each edge on the next 2 right-side rows—9 stitches. Work even until the piece measures 16" (40.5cm) from the beginning. Cut the yarn, leaving a 20" (51cm) tail for seaming. Do not bind off stitches; instead, thread the tail through the remaining stitches and pull tight. Thread the beginning tail through the cast-on stitches and pull tight.

FINISHING

Poke the coat hanger hook through the center of the Cover fabric, and slide the gathered end of the fabric over one end of the hanger. Using the yarn tail and mattress stitch (page 62), and working toward the cast-on edge, sew the long edges of the fabric together underneath the hanger. Sew the cast-on edge closed. Weave in ends.

TWINKLE KNIT BIT
KEEPING A NEEDLE GAUGE—A SMALL, FLAT PLASTIC OR METAL TOOL PERFORATED WITH HOLES IN THE DIAMETERS OF THE VARIOUS NEEDLE SIZES—WILL HELP YOU POSITIVELY IDENTIFY THOSE NEEDLES WHOSE SIZES HAVE BEEN ABRADED FROM THE NEEDLE BARRELS BY USE. KEEP CIRCULAR NEEDLES NEAT AND CORRECTLY IDENTIFIED BY STORING THEM IN CLEAR, SELF-SEALING PLASTIC BAGS THAT YOU'VE LABELED WITH A PERMANENT MARKER.

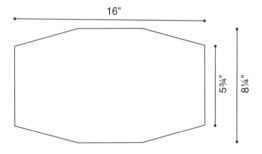

16"

5¾"

8¼"

saturday
morning:

fun
alfresco

Dramatic effects can be achieved through simple means—in this case, a straight-forward rib. The ribs provide elasticity needed for a good fit and depth to make the folded edge of the hat truly three-dimensional. It needs no fancy stitches to be eye-catching. Slip your work onto double-pointed needles to keep knitting at the crown of the hat.

snowcap hat PAGE 34

SIZE
One Size

KNITTED MEASUREMENTS
18" (51cm) circumference x 22" (56cm) long

MATERIALS

 super bulky

2 hanks Twinkle Handknits Soft Chunky, 100% virgin merino wool, 7 oz/200g, 83 yds/75m, #08 White

US size 17 (12.75mm) 16" (40cm) circular needle and double-pointed needles or size needed to obtain gauge

Stitch marker

Tapestry needle

GAUGE
12½ stitches and 14 rows = 7" (18cm) in k2, p2 rib (see page 59), slightly stretched

TAKE THE TIME TO CHECK YOUR GAUGE.

NOTES
The hat is knit in the round. Begin with the circular needle, and change to double-pointed needles when necessary.

HAT

With the circular needle, cast on 36 stitches. Place marker and join, being careful not to twist stitches.

RNDS 1–38: K1, *p2, k2; repeat from * to last 3 stitches, p2, k1.

RND 39 (DECREASE RND): K1, p2, k2, p1, k2tog, k1, p2, k2, p2, k1, ssk, p1, k2, p2, k1, ssk, p1, k2, p2, k2, p1, k2tog—32 stitches.

RNDS 40, 42, AND 44: Work stitches as they appear (knit the knits and purl the purls).

RND 41 (DECREASE RND): K1, p1, k2tog, k1, p1, k2, p1, k2tog, k1, p2, k2, p1, k1, ssk, p1, k2, p1, k1, ssk, p1, k2, p1, k1—28 stitches.

RND 43 (DECREASE RND): K1, p1, k2, k2tog, k1, p1, k2, p1, k2tog, k1, p1, k2, p1, k1, ssk, k2, p1, k1, ssk, k1—24 stitches

RND 45 (DECREASE RND): K1, k2tog, k3, k2tog, k1, p1, k2, k2tog, k1, p1, k3, ssk, k3—20 stitches.

Cut the yarn, leaving a 10" (25.5cm) tail. Thread the yarn through the remaining stitches and pull it tight. Weave in ends.

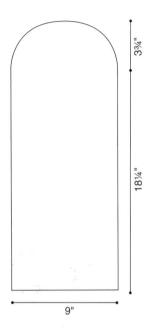

3¾"

18¼"

9"

TWINKLE KNIT BIT

AT LOOSE ENDS? SOONER OR LATER, YOU'LL NEED TO JOIN BALLS OF YARN. TRY TO DO SO AT THE BEGINNING OF A ROW TO AVOID A NOTICEABLE BUMP IN THE MIDDLE OF YOUR WORK. HERE IS ONE METHOD: TIE A SLIPKNOT IN THE NEW YARN AND TUCK THE END OF THE OLD YARN THROUGH THE LOOP. HOW CAN YOU TELL IF ENOUGH YARN REMAINS TO WORK A WHOLE ROW? IF YOU HAVE ABOUT THREE TIMES THE WIDTH OF YOUR PIECE REMAINING ON THE OLD SKEIN, YOU SHOULD HAVE ENOUGH YARN. IF NOT, START THE ROW FROM A NEW BALL. WITH CHUNKY WOOL YARNS, YOU ALSO CAN THREAD A DARNING NEEDLE WITH THE END OF THE OLD SKEIN AND SEW IT THROUGH THE MIDDLE OF A COUPLE INCHES OF THE BEGINNING END OF THE NEW SKEIN. OR, SIMPLY UNRAVEL THE FIBERS OF THE TWO ENDS TO BE JOINED, ENMESH AND MOISTEN THEM, AND THEN BRISKLY ROLL THE JOIN BETWEEN YOUR PALMS. THE FIBERS WILL FELT TOGETHER UNDER THE PRESSURE, HEAT, AND MOISTURE, FORMING A SECURE, SEAMLESS BOND.

For this pattern, you'll hold a loop of yarn on your left thumb and secure it with a "knit 2 together" (k2tog) stitch to form a loopy fringe used on either end. The body of the scarf features an overall pattern made from seed stitch, in which you work alternating knit and purl stitches and then purl the knit stitches and knit the purl stitches on successive rows. The regular, even-textured expanse of the scarf contrasts nicely with the organic, petal-like fringe.

peony scarf PAGE 34

SIZE
One Size

KNITTED MEASUREMENTS
7" x 53" (18cm x 134.5cm)

MATERIALS
 super bulky

2 hanks Twinkle Handknits Soft Chunky, 100% virgin merino wool, 7 oz/200g, 83 yds/75m, #17 Dusty Rose

US size 19 (15mm) needles

US size 17 (12.75mm) needles or size needed to obtain gauge

Stitch holder

Tapestry needle

GAUGE
7 stitches and 8 rows = 4" (10cm) in seed stitch (see page 59) on size 17 (12.75mm) needles

TAKE THE TIME TO CHECK YOUR GAUGE.

ABBREVIATION
ML (make loop) — Knit the next stitch, leaving the stitch on the left-hand needle; bring the yarn forward between the needles and around the left thumb to form a loop of about 1½" (3.8cm) in length (illus. 1), then back between the needles; knit the same stitch and slip it off the left-hand needle (illus. 2); slip the 2 stitches just made to the left-hand needle and knit 2 together through the back loops (illus. 3).

TWINKLE KNIT BIT
WRAP A BUNDLE OF HERBS, SUCH AS ROSEMARY OR LAVENDER, IN MUSLIN OR CHEESECLOTH, AND SLIP IT INTO YOUR STASH OF YARN OR AMONG YOUR KNITS (FOR EXAMPLE, OUT-OF-SEASON GARMENTS LIKE SCARVES AND HATS) TO FEND OFF INSECTS SUCH AS MOTHS THAT FIND YARN AND SWEATERS DELECTABLE.

SCARF

With the larger needles, cast on 9 stitches.

ROWS 1, 3, 5, 7, AND 9 (RS): ML in each stitch across.

ROWS 2, 4, 6, AND 8: Purl.

ROW 10: Change to the smaller needles and purl, increasing 4 stitches evenly across—13 stitches.

Work in seed stitch until the seed stitch portion of the Scarf measures 44" (112cm), ending with a wrong-side row. Place the stitches on a holder.

With the larger needles, cast on 9 stitches. Work rows 1–10.

Slip the stitches on the holder back to one of the smaller needles. With the right sides together and using the second smaller needle, join these stitches to the Scarf using the three-needle bind-off technique (page 63). Weave in ends.

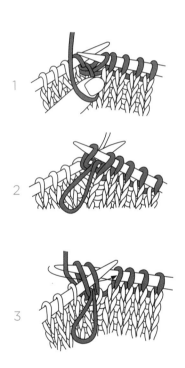

1

2

3

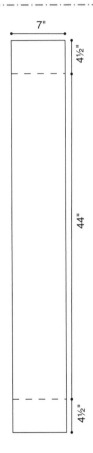

7"

4½"

44"

4½"

borealis sweater PAGE 36

SIZE
S (M, L)

REMEMBER TO USE THIS GUIDE TO FIND YOUR SIZE BASED ON YOUR ACTUAL BUST MEASUREMENT: S = 34"–36" (86cm–91cm); M = 37"–39" (94cm–99cm); L = 40"–42" (102cm–107cm).

KNITTED MEASUREMENTS
Bust: 30 (33, 35)" (76 [84, 89]cm)

Back length (not including collar): 22 (23, 23)" (56 [58.5, 58.5]cm)

MATERIALS

 super bulky

2 hanks Twinkle Handknits Soft Chunky, 100% virgin merino wool, 7 oz/200g, 83 yds/75m, #09 Black (A)

2 hanks #06 Baby Pink (B)

2 hanks #04 Coral (C)

2 hanks #19 Cream (D)

US size 19 (15mm) 29" (75cm) circular needle or size needed to obtain gauge

Stitch holders

Stitch markers

Tapestry needle

GAUGE
11 stitches and 16 rows = 7" (18cm) in reverse stockinette stitch (see page 59)

TAKE THE TIME TO CHECK YOUR GAUGE.

NOTES
The Sleeves are first knit flat, then the Body is knit in the round. The Sleeves are joined to the Body at the underarm, and the sweater is knit in one piece from this point. The front neckline is formed by short rows. Working the short rows will result in one stripe being two rows wider than the others in back. The stitch marker at the beginning of the round should be a different color from the others. The entire piece is worked in stockinette stitch, then turned inside out to use the "wrong" side as the right side. The knit rows will be identified as right-side rows for the purpose of the knitting only.

Borders between the colors are accented with dashed lines that result from using the wrong side of the stockinette stitch as the right side. The sleeves are slightly belled, and the shoulder seams are discreetly worked with short-row shaping for a refined silhouette. The Soft Chunky yarn has enough give to allow the negative ease—knitted measurements that are smaller than your body measurements—to provide a sleek and snug fit.

STRIPE PATTERN

6 rows/rounds each of B, C, D, and A

LEFT SLEEVE

With A, cast on 23 stitches. Knit 4 rows—2 ridges.
Change to stockinette stitch and work even for
2 rows. Continue stockinette stitch and begin the
stripe pattern. Work even for 7 more rows.

NEXT ROW (WS): K9, k2tog, k2, ssk, k8—21 stitches.
Work even for 11 more rows.

NEXT ROW (WS): K1, ssk, knit to last 3 stitches,
k2tog, k1—19 stitches.

Work even for 10 (12, 12) rows.

UNDERARM SHAPING

Bind off 2 stitches at the beginning of the next
row and 1 stitch at the beginning of the following
row. Place the remaining 16 stitches on a holder.

RIGHT SLEEVE

Work as for the Left Sleeve up to the underarm
shaping step.

UNDERARM SHAPING

Bind off 1 stitch at the beginning of the next
row and 2 stitches at the beginning of the
following row. Place the remaining 16 stitches
on a holder.

TWINKLE KNIT BIT
IF YOU'RE TRYING TO KEEP TRACK OF SEVERAL
PLACES IN YOUR KNITTING PATTERN AND LACK KNIT-
TING MARKERS IN CONTRASTING COLORS, TIE LOOPS
OF YARN TO YOUR STITCH MARKERS TO DISTINGUISH
THEM FROM ONE ANOTHER.

BODY

With A, cast on 24 (26, 28) stitches, place marker,
cast on 24 (26, 28) stitches, place marker to
indicate the beginning of the round—48 (52, 56)
stitches. Join, being careful not to twist stitches.
Work 4 rounds in garter stitch (knit 1 round,
purl 1 round). Change to stockinette stitch and
work even for 2 rounds.

Continue in stockinette stitch and begin the
stripe pattern. Work even until 1 (3, 3) rounds of
the second C stripe is worked, ending 1 stitch
before the end of the last round.

DIVIDE THE BODY

Removing the markers as you work, bind off
2 stitches, knit to 1 stitch before the marker, bind
off 2 stitches, knit to end of round—22 (24, 26)
stitches each for the front and back. Body
measures approximately 16 (17, 17)" (40.5 [43,
43]cm) from the beginning.

JOIN THE SLEEVES AND BODY

Maintaining the established stripe pattern, k16
Left Sleeve stitches, place marker, k22 (24, 26) front
stitches, place marker, k16 Right Sleeve stitches,
place marker, k22 (24, 26) back stitches, place
marker to indicate the beginning of the round—
76 (80, 84) stitches. Work 1 (2, 2) round(s) even.

RAGLAN SHAPING

**NOTE: READ ALL SHAPING INSTRUCTIONS BEFORE
BEGINNING.**

NEXT RND (DECREASE RND): ★K1, k2tog, knit to 3
stitches before the marker, ssk, k1, slip marker;
repeat from ★ around—68 (72, 76) stitches.
Repeat Decrease Rnd every 3 rounds 2 (1, 2)
more times, then every other round 0 (2, 1)
time(s). Work even for 4 rounds.

SIZE S AND L ONLY: Repeat Decrease Rnd.

SIZE M ONLY: Decrease on the Sleeves only.

ALL SIZES: *At the same time*, when 8 (9, 10) rounds of the raglan shaping are complete, work 2 short rows as follows, maintaining the raglan shaping:

★Work to 4 stitches before the center front, wrap and turn (page 63); repeat from ★. Continue on all stitches, picking up the wraps as you come to them—44 stitches remain when all shaping is complete.

COLLAR

Continuing in the established stripe pattern, work even until the collar measures approximately 14" (35.5cm), ending with 6 rounds of A. Bind off loosely.

FINISHING

Turn the sweater inside out so that the purl side becomes the right side. With the right side facing and using mattress stitch (page 62), sew the Sleeve and underarm seams. Weave in ends on the wrong side.

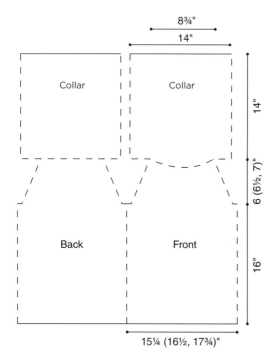

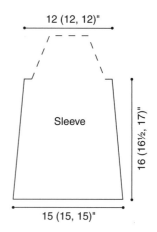

tidepool sweater

PAGE 38

Unlike a sweater with set-in sleeves, the Tidepool Sweater relies on a favorite construction technique: knitting the gently belled sleeves flat and then joining them at the underarm to the snug body, which has been knitted in the round. The remainder of the garment is then knitted as a whole on circular needles, creating a yoke. Raglan shaping to the neckline yields a comfortable shoulder. This design feature minimizes the seaming—you have to seam only the underside of the sleeves and the underarm.

SIZE
S (M, L)

REMEMBER TO USE THIS GUIDE TO FIND YOUR SIZE BASED ON YOUR ACTUAL BUST MEASUREMENT: S = 34″–36″ (86cm–91cm); M = 37″–39″ (94cm–99cm); L = 40″–42″ (102cm–107cm).

KNITTED MEASUREMENTS
Bust: 28 (30½, 33)″ (71 [77.5, 84]cm)

Back length (not including neck trim): 23 (24, 26)″ (58.5 [61, 66]cm)

MATERIALS
 super bulky

2 (3, 3) hanks Twinkle Handknits Soft Chunky, 100% virgin merino wool, 7 oz/200g, 83 yds/75m, #11 Clover (A)

2 (3, 3) hanks #20 Icy Blue (B)

US size 19 (15mm) 16″ (40cm) and 29″ (75cm) circular needles or size needed to obtain gauge

Stitch holders

Stitch markers

Tapestry needle

GAUGE
11 stitches and 16 rows = 7″ (18cm) in stockinette stitch (see page 59)

TAKE THE TIME TO CHECK YOUR GAUGE.

NOTES
The Sleeves are first knit flat, then the Body is knit in the round. The Sleeves are joined to the Body at the underarm, and the sweater is knit in one piece from this point. The front neckline is formed by short rows. Change to the shorter needle when necessary. The stitch marker at the beginning of the round should be a different color from the others.

STRIPE PATTERN

6 rows/rounds B, 6 rows/rounds A.

LEFT SLEEVE

With the longer needle and A, cast on 23 stitches. Knit 6 rows in garter stitch—3 ridges.

With B, begin stockinette stitch and the stripe pattern. Work even for 8 rows.
NEXT ROW (RS): With A, k1, ssk, knit to last 3 stitches, k2tog, k1—21 stitches.

Work even for 11 rows.
NEXT ROW (RS): With A, k8, k2tog, k1, ssk, k8—19 stitches.

Work even for 9 (11, 11) rows.

UNDERARM SHAPING

Bind off 2 stitches at the beginning of the next row and 1 stitch at the beginning of the following row. Place the remaining 16 stitches on a holder.

RIGHT SLEEVE

Work as for the Left Sleeve up to the underarm shaping step.

UNDERARM SHAPING

Bind off 1 stitch at the beginning of the next row and 2 stitches at the beginning of the following row. Place the remaining 16 stitches on a holder.

TWINKLE KNIT BIT

WHEN CASTING ON OR BINDING OFF AT NECK EDGES, USE NEEDLES A SIZE LARGER OR USE TWO NEEDLES HELD TOGETHER. DOING SO CREATES SLACK THAT MAKES NECK OPENINGS EASIER TO NEGOTIATE.

BODY

With the longer needle and A, cast on 28 (30, 32) stitches, place marker to indicate the right underarm, cast on 28 (30, 32) stitches, place marker to indicate the left underarm and the beginning of the round—56 (60, 64) stitches. Join, being careful not to twist stitches. Work 6 rounds in garter stitch (knit 1 round, purl 1 round).

With B, begin stockinette stitch (knit all rounds) and the stripe pattern. Knit 1 round.
*NEXT RND (FRONT DECREASE RND): Ssk, knit to 2 stitches before the marker, k2tog, slip marker, knit to the end of the round—54 (58, 62) stitches. Work even for 5 rounds.
NEXT RND (BACK DECREASE RND): Knit to the marker, slip marker, k2tog, knit to 2 stitches before the marker, ssk—52 (56, 60) stitches. ****** Work even for 4 rounds.

Repeat from * once, then repeat from * to ** once—44 (48, 52) stitches. Work even for 1 (3, 3) round(s), ending the last round 1 stitch before the beginning-of-round marker.

DIVIDE THE BODY

Removing markers as you work, bind off 2 stitches, knit to 1 stitch before the marker, bind off 2 stitches, knit to end of round—20 (22, 24) stitches each for the front and back.

JOIN THE SLEEVES AND BODY

Maintaining the established stripe pattern, k16 Left Sleeve stitches, place marker, k20 (22, 24) front stitches, place marker, k16 Right Sleeve stitches, place marker, k20 (22, 24) back stitches, place marker to indicate the beginning of the round—72 (76, 80) stitches. Work 2 rounds even.

RAGLAN SHAPING

NOTE: READ ALL SHAPING INSTRUCTIONS BEFORE BEGINNING.

NEXT RND (DECREASE RND): *K1, k2tog, knit to 3 stitches before the marker, ssk, k1, slip marker; repeat from * around—64 (68, 72) stitches. Repeat Decrease Rnd every 3 rounds 4 (3, 4) more times and every other round 1 (2, 1) time(s)—24 (28, 32) stitches. Knit 1 (2, 2) round(s).

SIZES M AND L ONLY: Knit 1 round, decreasing on the front and back stitches only.

At the same time, when 14 (15, 16) rounds of the raglan shaping are complete, work short rows as follows, maintaining the raglan shaping:

*Work to 6 stitches before the center front, wrap and turn (see the short-row instructions on page 63); repeat from *. Continue on all stitches, picking up the wraps—24 (24, 28) stitches remain when all shaping is complete.

Slip 4 Left Sleeve stitches to the right-hand needle. Cut the yarn.

NECK BAND

With B, cast on 20 stitches, knit 24 (24, 28) neck stitches, cable cast on 20 stitches, turn—64 (64, 68) stitches. Working back and forth, knit 8 rows—4 ridges. Bind off.

FINISHING

Sew the Sleeve and underarm seams. Weave in ends.

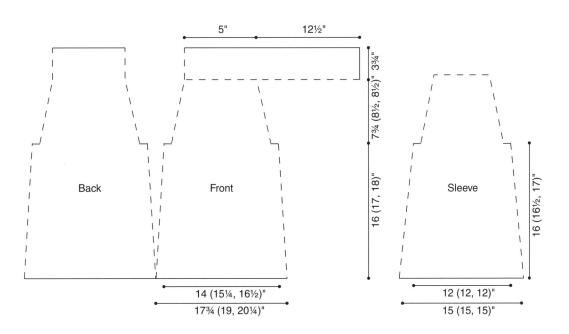

oceania sweater PAGE 38

SIZE
S (M, L)

REMEMBER TO USE THIS GUIDE TO FIND YOUR SIZE BASED ON YOUR ACTUAL BUST MEASUREMENT: S = 34"–36" (86cm–91cm); M = 37"–39" (94cm–99cm); L = 40"–42" (102cm–107cm).

KNITTED MEASUREMENTS
Bust: 30½ (33, 35)" (77.5 [84, 89]cm)

Back length: 21 (21, 22)" (53.5 [53.5, 56]cm)

MATERIALS

 super bulky

3 (3, 4) hanks Twinkle Handknits Soft Chunky, 100% virgin merino wool, 7 oz/200g, 83 yds/75m, #12 Riviera (A)

1 hank #08 White (B)

US size 19 (15mm) 29" (75cm) circular needle or size needed to obtain gauge

Stitch holders

Stitch markers

Tapestry needle

Size J-10 (6mm) crochet hook

GAUGE
11 stitches and 16 rows = 7" (18cm) in stockinette stitch (see page 59)

TAKE THE TIME TO CHECK YOUR GAUGE.

NOTES
The Sleeves are first knit flat, then the Body is knit in the round. The Sleeves are joined to the Body at the underarm, and the sweater is knit in one piece from this point. The front neckline is formed by short rows. Work the first stitch at each neck edge in garter stitch. The stitch marker at the beginning of the round should be a different color from the others.

Like the Tidepool Sweater (page 91), the Oceania Sweater has sleeves that are knit flat and then joined to the body at the underarm. The rest of the sweater is then knitted on circular needles. Short rows allow you create a split front collar, and yarn overs form eyelets for the crocheted lace tie. The raglan shaping on the shoulder has some give, offering the ease of movement you need for your getaway weekend activities.

ABBREVIATIONS

Inc 1—Knit 1 in the row below the next stitch, knit the next stitch.

WS Decrease Row—*Purl to 3 stitches before the marker, ssp, p1, slip marker, p1, p2tog; repeat from * 3 times, purl to the end.

RS Decrease Row—*Knit to 3 stitches before the marker, k2tog, k1, slip marker, k1, ssk; repeat from * 3 times, knit to the end.

LEFT SLEEVE

With A, cast on 13 (13, 15) stitches. Work 2 rows in k1, p1 rib (page 59).

Change to stockinette stitch and work even for 10 (8, 10) rows.

NEXT ROW (INCREASE ROW): K1, inc 1, knit to the last 2 stitches, inc 1, k1.

Repeat Increase Row every 10 (8, 10) rows twice more—19 (19, 21) stitches.

SIZE M ONLY: Work 5 rows even; repeat Increase Row once more—21 stitches.

ALL SIZES: Work even until the Sleeve measures 15" (38cm) from the beginning, ending with a right-side row.

UNDERARM SHAPING

Bind off 2 stitches at the beginning of the next row and 1 stitch at the beginning of the following row. Place the remaining 16 (18, 18) stitches on a holder.

RIGHT SLEEVE

Work as for the Left Sleeve up to the underarm shaping step.

UNDERARM SHAPING

Bind off 1 stitch at the beginning of the next row and 2 stitches at the beginning of the following row. Place the remaining 16 (18, 18) stitches on a holder.

BODY

With A, cast on 11 (12, 13) stitches, place marker to indicate the right underarm, cast on 22 (24, 26) stitches, place marker to indicate the left underarm, cast on 11 (12, 13) stitches, place marker to indicate the center of the front and the beginning of the round—44 (48, 52) stitches. Join, being careful not to twist stitches. Work 2 rounds in k1, p1 rib.

Change to stockinette stitch and work 7 rounds even.

NEXT RND (BACK INCREASE RND): Knit to the right underarm marker, slip marker, k1, inc 1, knit to the left underarm marker, inc 1, slip marker, knit to end of round—46 (50, 54) stitches. Work 7 rounds even.

NEXT RND (FRONT INCREASE RND): Knit to 1 stitch before the right underarm marker, inc 1, slip marker, knit to the left underarm marker, slip marker, k1, inc 1, knit to end of round—48 (52, 56) stitches.

Work even until the Body measures 12" (30.5cm) from the beginning.

DIVIDE THE BODY

*Removing the markers as you work, knit to 1 stitch before the marker, bind off 2 stitches; repeat from * once, work to end of round—22 (24, 26) stitches each for front and back.

JOIN THE SLEEVES AND BODY AND DIVIDE FOR THE NECK

K11 (12, 13) front stitches, place marker for the raglan shaping, k16 (18, 18) Right Sleeve stitches, place marker for the raglan shaping, k22 (24, 26) back stitches, place marker for raglan shaping, k16 (18, 18) Left Sleeve stitches, place marker for the raglan shaping, k11 (12, 13) front stitches, turn—76 (84, 88) stitches.

NEXT ROW: K1, purl to the last stitch, k1.

RAGLAN SHAPING, NECK SHAPING, AND EYELETS

NOTE: READ ALL INSTRUCTIONS IN THIS SECTION BEFORE BEGINNING.

EYELET ROW (RS): K2, yo, ssk, work in established pattern to the last 4 stitches, k2tog, yo, k2. Keeping each edge stitch in garter stitch, repeat Eyelet Row every 6th row twice more.

At the same time, working RS or WS Decrease Rows as appropriate, decrease on the next row, then every 3 rows 5 (4, 5) more times—28 (44, 40) stitches remaining.

SIZE S ONLY: Work 1 row even. Work 1 more row, decreasing on the front and back stitches only—24 stitches.

SIZE M ONLY: Work 1 row even. Work 1 row, decreasing on the back stitches only. Work 1 row, decreasing on the Sleeve stitches only. Work 1 row, decreasing on the front and back stitches only. Work 1 row even. Repeat Decrease Row—26 stitches.

SIZE L ONLY: Work 1 row even. Work 1 row, decreasing on the front and back stitches only. Work 1 row, decreasing on the Sleeve stitches only. Work 1 row, decreasing on the front and back stitches only—28 stitches.

ALL SIZES: *At the same time*, when 14 rows of the raglan shaping are complete, work short rows as follows, maintaining the raglan shaping: Work to 4 stitches from the left front edge, wrap and turn (see page 63); work to 4 stitches from the right front edge, wrap and turn; work to 6 stitches from the left front edge, wrap and turn; work to 6 stitches from the right front edge, wrap and turn. Continue on all stitches, picking up all the wraps—24 (26, 28) stitches remain when all shaping is complete. Work 4 rows in k1, p1 rib. Bind off loosely.

FINISHING

Sew the Sleeve and underarm seams. Weave in ends.

With a crochet hook and B, chain 40" (101.5cm); fasten off. Using the photo as a guide, thread the chain through the eyelets.

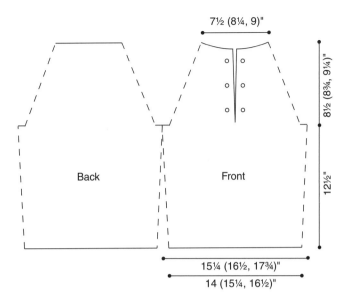

7½ (8¼, 9)"

8½ (8¾, 9¼)"

12½"

Back

Front

15¼ (16½, 17¾)"

14 (15¼, 16½)"

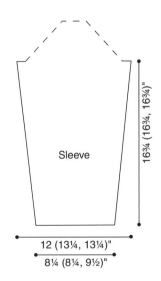

16¾ (16¾, 16¾)"

Sleeve

12 (13¼, 13¼)"

8¼ (8¼, 9½)"

Perfect as gifts, these iPod sleeves are worked on small needles in stock-inette stitch with rib-bing at the opening. Knitting doesn't get much easier than this: The body, which features panels of muted colors con-trasted with surpris-ing accent tones in a soft, cushioning silk-and-cotton yarn, is a rectangle that you simply fold over and seam on two sides. Team up white and black yarns for another classic Twinkle color combination.

equator iPod sleeves

PAGE 38

SIZE
One Size

KNITTED MEASUREMENTS
3″ x 4½″ (7.5cm x 11.5cm)

MATERIALS

 fine

1 ball Twinkle Handknits Cruise, 70% silk/30% cotton, 1¾ oz/50g, 120 yds/109m, #68 Stone Grey (A)

1 ball #63 Chili (B)

or

1 ball #71 Peanut (A)

1 ball #67 Navy (B)

US size 6 (4mm) needles or size needed to obtain gauge

Tapestry needle

GAUGE
24 stitches and 30 rows = 4″ (10cm) in stockinette stitch (see page 59)

TAKE THE TIME TO CHECK YOUR GAUGE.

SLEEVE

With A, cast on 33 stitches. Work even in stockinette stitch until the piece measures 3" (7.5cm) from the beginning. Change to B and work even until the piece measures 4" (10cm) from the beginning. Work in k1, p1 rib for ½" (13mm). Bind off loosely.

FINISHING

Fold the piece in half, and sew the side and bottom seams. Weave in ends.

TWINKLE KNIT BIT

TUCK AN EMERY BOARD INTO YOUR KNITTING KIT TO HELP KEEP YOUR FINGERNAILS SMOOTH (AND THE POINTS OF DAMAGED WOODEN NEEDLES TOO) AND THUS PREVENT YARN SNAGS. DOFF THOSE RINGS AND BRACELETS THAT CAN CATCH LOOPS OF YARN AS WELL. SAVE THEM FOR THE DEBUT OF YOUR FINISHED KNITS.

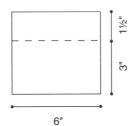

This intarsia motif is simple to do and adds a jolt of color to the Northern Cross sweater. Just before the intarsia section, you'll need to knit rows back and forth to make the cross intarsia motif. Then you'll work in the round once again to form the funnel neck. At the sweater's lower edge, you'll pick up stitches to purl, giving the hem a distinctive raised detail that both contrasts with the stockinette above it and prevents the hem from rolling.

northern cross
sweater PAGE 40

SIZE
S (M, L)

REMEMBER TO USE THIS GUIDE TO FIND YOUR SIZE BASED ON YOUR ACTUAL BUST MEASUREMENT: S = 34"–36" (86cm–91cm); M = 37"–39" (94cm–99cm); L = 40"–42" (102cm–107cm).

KNITTED MEASUREMENTS
Bust: 30 (33, 35)" (76 [84, 89]cm)

MATERIALS
 super bulky

5 (5, 5) hanks Twinkle Handknits Soft Chunky, 100% virgin merino wool, 7 oz/200g, 83 yds/75m, #18 French Grey (A)

1 hank #04 Coral (B)

US size 19 (15mm) 29" (75cm) circular needles or size needed to obtain gauge

US size 19 (15mm) double-pointed needles or size needed to obtain gauge

Stitch holders

Stitch markers

Tapestry needle

GAUGE
11 stitches and 16 rows = 7" (18cm) in stockinette stitch (see page 59)

TAKE THE TIME TO CHECK YOUR GAUGE.

NOTES
The Sleeves are first knit flat. The Body is started in two pieces and then joined and worked in the round to the underarm. The Body and Sleeves are worked back and forth when the Sleeves are joined. After the intarsia work, the sweater is worked in the round. The front neckline is formed by short rows. Two stitch markers should be a different color from the others to indicate the chart stitches. Change to double-pointed needles when necessary.

ABBREVIATIONS

Inc 1—Knit 1 in the row below the next stitch, knit the next stitch.

RS Decrease Row—K2, ssk, *knit to 3 stitches before the marker, k2tog, k1, slip marker, k1, ssk; repeat from * 2 times, knit to 4 stitches from the end, k2tog, k2.

WS Decrease Row—P2, p2tog, *purl to 3 stitches before the marker, ssp, p1, slip marker, p1, p2tog; repeat from * 2 times, purl to 4 stitches from the end, ssp, purl 2.

LEFT SLEEVE

With the circular needle and A, cast on 17 (19, 21) stitches. Work even in stockinette stitch until the Sleeve measures approximately 10" (25.5cm), ending with a wrong-side row.

NEXT ROW (INCREASE ROW): K1, inc 1, knit to the last 2 stitches, inc 1, k1—19 (21, 23) stitches. Work even until the Sleeve measures 13" (33cm) from the beginning, ending with a wrong-side row.

UNDERARM SHAPING

Bind off 2 stitches at the beginning of the next row and 1 stitch at the beginning of the following row. Place the remaining 16 (18, 20) stitches on a holder.

RIGHT SLEEVE

Work as for the Left Sleeve up to the underarm shaping step.

UNDERARM SHAPING

Bind off 1 stitch at the beginning of the next row and 2 stitches at the beginning of the following row. Place the remaining 16 (18, 20) stitches on a holder.

FRONT

With the circular needle and A, using the long-tail method, cast on 14 (16, 18) stitches. Work 2 rows in stockinette stitch, beginning with a wrong-side row. Continue in stockinette stitch, and cast on 1 stitch at the beginning of the next 2 rows, 2 stitches at the beginning of the next 2 rows, and 3 stitches at the beginning of the following 2 rows—26 (28, 30) stitches. Place the Front stitches on a holder.

BACK

Work as for the Front; do not place the Back stitches on a holder.

JOIN THE FRONT AND BACK

NOTE: READ ALL INSTRUCTIONS IN THIS SECTION BEFORE CONTINUING.

Place marker to indicate the beginning of the round. Using yarn from the Back, knit the Front stitches from the holder, place marker to indicate the right underarm, knit to end of round—52 (56, 60) stitches.

Knit 9 rounds even.

NEXT RND (DECREASE RND): *K1, ssk, knit to 3 stitches before the marker, k2tog, k1, slip marker; repeat from * once—48 (52, 56) stitches. Knit 10 rounds, ending the last round 1 stitch before end of round.

DIVIDE THE BODY AND BEGIN THE CHART

Removing the markers as you work, bind off 2 stitches (1 stitch on the right-hand needle), k4 (5, 6), place marker to indicate the beginning of the chart stitches, work row 1 of the chart across the next 12 stitches, place marker to indicate the end of the chart stitches, k5 (6, 7), bind off 2 stitches, knit to end of round, cast on 1 stitch, turn—22 (24, 26) stitches for the Front and 23 (25, 27) stitches for the Back. Continue working the intarsia chart on subsequent rows.

JOIN THE SLEEVES AND BODY

With the wrong side facing, p23 (25, 27) Back stitches, place marker for the raglan shaping, p16 (18, 20) Right Sleeve stitches from holder, p22 (24, 26) Front stitches, place marker for the raglan shaping, p16 (18, 20) Left Sleeve stitches from holder, cast on 1 stitch—78 (86, 94) stitches.
NOTE: THE STITCHES CAST ON AT EACH EDGE WILL BE USED FOR SEAMING LATER.

Working back and forth in stockinette stitch, work 2 (1, 1) more row(s).

RAGLAN SHAPING AND FRONT NECK SHAPING
NOTE: READ ALL INSTRUCTIONS IN THIS SECTION BEFORE BEGINNING.
Work a Decrease Row on the next row, then every fourth row 1 (0, 0) time, then every third row 4 (5, 5) times, working RS or WS Decrease Rows as appropriate.
SIZE M ONLY: Work even 2 rows. Work 1 row, decreasing on the Back and Sleeve stitches only.
SIZE L ONLY: Work 1 row even. Work 1 row, decreasing on the Front and Back stitches only. Work 1 row even; repeat Decrease Row.

At the same time, when the intarsia chart is complete, continuing with A, bind off 1 stitch at the beginning of the next (wrong-side) row, work to end of row. Do not remove chart stitch markers.
NEXT ROW (RS): Bind off 1 stitch at the beginning of the row, work to end of row, do not turn. Join and begin working in the round, continuing the raglan shaping.

NEXT RND: Work to 4 stitches past the beginning-of-chart marker, wrap and turn, work to 4 stitches past the end-of-chart marker, wrap and turn (page 63), work to end of round, picking up the wraps as you come to them.

Continue working on all stitches until the raglan shaping is complete—28 (30, 32) stitches remain.

COLLAR
Work even for 12 more rounds. Bind off loosely.

LOWER BAND
With the right side facing and using A, pick up and knit 52 (56, 50) stitches around the lower edge. Place marker to indicate the beginning of round. Purl 3 rounds. Bind off loosely purlwise.

FINISHING
Sew the Sleeve, raglan, and underarm seams. Weave in ends.

TWINKLE KNIT BIT
WHEN REACHING A POINT WHERE YOU'LL CHANGE COLORS IN AN INTARSIA SECTION, HOLD THE OLD COLOR TO THE LEFT WHEN YOU PICK UP THE NEW ONE (ILLUS. 1 AND 2). THIS WILL TWIST THE YARNS TO CONNECT THE TWO COLORED SECTIONS NEATLY AND PREVENT A HOLE. ALIGNING ROWS OF STITCHES IN THE INTARSIA SECTIONS AND BLOCKING YOUR FINISHED GARMENT WILL SMOOTH THE TRANSITIONS BETWEEN COLORS.

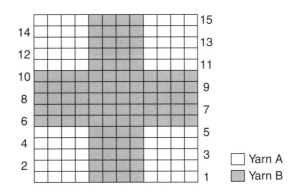

☐	Yarn A	
▨	Yarn B	

WORKING INTARSIA

1   2

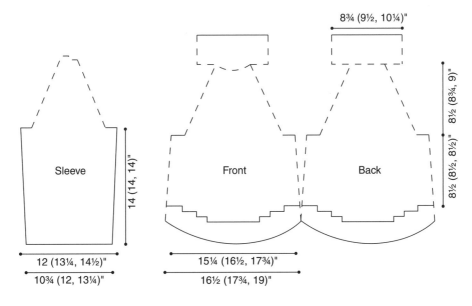

8¾ (9½, 10¼)"

Sleeve

14 (14, 14)"

Front

Back

8½ (8¾, 9)"

8½ (8½, 8½)"

12 (13¼, 14½)"

10¾ (12, 13¼)"

15¼ (16½, 17¾)"

16½ (17¾, 19)"

The Urchin Beret is made in one piece on circular needles, but yarn overs and slipped stitches create a pretty pattern of nine panels that are roughly parallelograms in shape. You'll begin the pattern on smaller needles to rib a lower band for the beret, but the hat is designed to fit loosely for a jaunty, boho look to add a soft, organic touch to a sleek outfit.

urchin beret PAGE 40

SIZE
One Size

KNITTED MEASUREMENTS
Circumference at brim: 20" (51m)

Diameter at widest point: 11$\frac{1}{4}$" (28cm)

MATERIALS
 super bulky

1 hank Twinkle Handknits Soft Chunky, 100% virgin merino wool, 7 oz/200g, 83 yds/75m, #26 Lilac

Set of 4 US size 19 (15mm) double-pointed needles or size needed to obtain gauge

Stitch marker

Tapestry needle

GAUGE
11 stitches and 16 rows = 7" (18cm) in stockinette stitch (see page 59)

TAKE THE TIME TO CHECK YOUR GAUGE.

TWINKLE KNIT BIT

KNITTING CAN LEAVE YOUR HANDS FEELING DRY, AND ROUGH YARNS CAN CHAFE. SOOTHE YOUR SKIN WITH A SMALL TUBE OF GREASELESS HAND CREAM. KNITTERS' FAVES INCLUDE BURT'S BEES HAND SALVE, WHICH COMES IN A TIN AND WON'T LEAK IN YOUR KNITTING BAG, AND UDDERLY SMOOTH UDDER CREAM. APPLYING CREAM ALSO GIVES YOUR HANDS A MOMENT'S REST AND A LITTLE MASSAGE.

BERET

Cast on 36 stitches. Divide stitches evenly between 3 needles. Place marker to indicate the beginning of the round. Join, being careful not to twist stitches. Work 4 rounds in k2, p2 rib.

RND 1: ★K4, yo; repeat from ★ around—45 stitches.

RND 2 AND ALL EVEN-NUMBERED RNDS: Knit.

RND 3: ★K5, yo; repeat from ★ around—54 stitches.

RND 5: ★K6, yo; repeat from ★ around—63 stitches.

RND 7: ★Ssk, k5; repeat from ★ around—54 stitches.

RND 9: ★Ssk, k4; repeat from ★ around—45 stitches.

RND 11: ★Ssk, k3; repeat from ★ around—36 stitches.

RND 13: ★Ssk, k2; repeat from ★ around—27 stitches.

RND 15: ★Ssk, k1; repeat from ★ around—18 stitches.

Cut the yarn, leaving a 12" (30.5cm) tail. Weave the tail through the remaining stitches, and pull it tight. Weave in ends.

KEY

☐ K on RS

⊙ yo

◺ SSK on RS

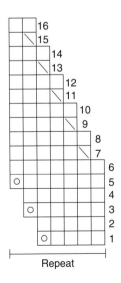

Repeat

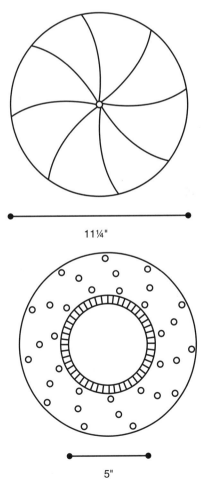

11¼"

5"

sunday
afternoon:
last night
away

Twinkle style is a study in contrasts, and this pattern illustrates the principle perfectly. The openwork in this sweater's wide funnel neck lends a lightness to contrast with the chunky yarn. Princess seams along the bust help the bulky yarn create a surprisingly flattering silhouette, and raglan sleeves lend a comfortable fit and allow ease of movement.

nimbus sweater PAGE 44

SIZE
S (M, L)

REMEMBER TO USE THIS GUIDE TO FIND YOUR SIZE BASED ON YOUR ACTUAL BUST MEASUREMENT: S = 34″–36″ (86cm–91cm); M = 37″–39″ (94cm–99cm); L = 40″–42″ (102cm–107cm).

KNITTED MEASUREMENTS
Bust: 29 (31, 34)″ (73.5 [78.5, 86.5]cm)

Back length (not including collar): 19 (20, 21¾)″ (48.5 [51, 55.5]cm)

MATERIALS

 super bulky

4 (4, 5) hanks Twinkle Handknits Soft Chunky, 100% virgin merino wool, 7 oz/200g, 83 yds/75m, #08 White

US size 19 (15mm) 29″ (75cm) and 24″ (60cm) circular needles or size needed to obtain gauge

Stitch holders

Stitch markers

Tapestry needle

GAUGE
11 stitches and 16 rows = 7″ (18cm) in stockinette stitch (see page 59)

TAKE THE TIME TO CHECK YOUR GAUGE.

ABBREVIATION
inc 1—Knit 1 in the row below the next stitch, knit the next stitch.

NOTES
The Sleeves are first knit flat, then the Body is knit in the round. The Sleeves are joined to the body at the underarm, and the sweater is knit in one piece from that point. The stitch marker at the beginning of the round should be a different color from the others. If you are unable to fit the stitches for the funnel neck onto the 24″ (60cm) circular needles, use double-pointed needles instead.

OPENWORK RIB PATTERN (MULTIPLE OF 4)

(See chart on page 111.)

RND 1: *K2, yo, ssk; repeat from *.

RND 2: *K2tog, yo, k2; repeat from *.

Repeat rounds 1 and 2 for pattern.

SLEEVES (MAKE 2)

With the longer needle, cast on 13 (15, 17) stitches. Work even in stockinette stitch for 10 rows.

INCREASE ROW (RS): K1, inc 1, knit to last 2 stitches, inc 1, k1—15 (17, 19) stitches.

Work even for 10 rows, then repeat Increase Row—17 (19, 21) stitches.

Work even until the Sleeve measures 13" (33cm) from the beginning, ending with a wrong-side row.

UNDERARM SHAPING

Bind off 2 stitches at the beginning of the next 2 rows. Place the remaining 13 (15, 17) stitches on a holder.

BODY

With longer needles, cast on 23 (25, 27) front stitches, place marker to indicate the right underarm, cast on 23 (25, 27) back stitches, place marker to indicate the left underarm and the beginning of the round—46 (50, 54) stitches. Join, being careful not to twist stitches.

RNDS 1–4: Knit.

RND 5: Knit across front stitches to the marker, slip marker, k3, k2tog, yo, k13 (15, 17), k2tog, yo, ssk, k3.

RND 6: Knit.

RND 7: K6, ssk, k7 (9, 11), k2tog, k6, slip marker, knit across the back stitches to end of round—44 (48, 52) stitches.

RND 8: Knit.

RND 9: Knit to the marker, slip marker, k2, k2tog, yo, k15 (17, 19), yo, ssk, k2.

RNDS 10 AND 11: Knit.

RND 12: K6, ssk, k5 (7, 9), k2tog, k6, slip marker, knit across the back stitches to end of round—42 (46, 50) stitches.

RND 13: Knit to the marker, slip marker, k1, k2tog, yo, k17 (19, 21), yo, ssk, k1.

RNDS 14–16: Knit.

RND 17: K6, ssk, k3 (5, 7), k2tog, k6, slip marker, k2tog, yo, k19 (21, 23), yo, ssk—40 (44, 48) stitches.

RNDS 18–20: Knit.

RND 21: K6, inc 1, k3 (5, 7), inc 1, k5, sl 1, remove marker, slip stitch back to the left-hand needle and k2tog, place marker, yo, k21 (23, 25), yo, sl 1, remove marker, slip stitch back to the left-hand needle, place marker, ssk—42 (46, 50) stitches.

RNDS 22–23: Knit.

RND 24: K6, inc 1, k5 (7, 9), inc 1, k6, slip marker, knit across the back stitches to end of round—44 (48, 52) stitches.

RND 25: Yo, ssk, knit to 2 stitches before the next marker, k2tog, yo, slip marker, k23 (25, 27).

RND 26: Knit.

RND 27: K6, inc 1, k7 (9, 11), inc 1, k6, slip marker, knit to end of round—46 (50, 54) stitches.

RND 28: Knit.

RND 29: K1, yo, ssk, knit to 3 stitches before the marker, k2tog, yo, k1, slip marker, knit to end of round.

RND 30: Knit, ending 2 stitches before end of round.

DIVIDE THE BODY

Removing markers as you work, bind off 4 stitches, knit to 2 stitches before the marker, bind off 4 stitches, knit to end of round—19 (21, 23) stitches each for front and back.

JOIN THE SLEEVES AND BODY

K13 (15, 17) Sleeve stitches from holder, place marker to indicate the raglan shaping, k19 (21, 23) front stitches, place marker to indicate the raglan shaping, k13 (15, 17) Sleeve stitches from holder, place marker to indicate the raglan shaping, k19 (21, 23) back stitches, place marker to indicate the raglan shaping and the beginning of the round—64 (72, 80) stitches. Work 2 (2, 3) rounds even.

RAGLAN SHAPING

NOTE: READ ALL SHAPING INSTRUCTIONS BEFORE BEGINNING.

NEXT RND (DECREASE RND): *K1, ssk, knit to 3 stitches before the marker, k2tog, k1, slip marker; repeat from * around—56 (64, 72) stitches. Repeat the Decrease Round every 3 rounds 2 (3, 3) more times—40 (40, 48) stitches. Work 2 (1, 2) rounds even.

NECK AND RAGLAN SHAPING

SIZES S AND L ONLY: K1, ssk, knit to the marker, remove marker, place the next 13 (–, 15) front neck stitches on a holder, turn, leaving the remainder of the round unworked.

NEXT ROW (WS): Bind off 3 (–, 4) stitches at the beginning of the row, purl to the marker, slip marker, p2tog, purl to 3 stitches before the marker, ssp, p1, slip marker, p2tog, purl to end, remove marker, turn—20 (–, 25) stitches. Bind off 3 (–, 4) stitches at the beginning of the

next 3 rows, do not turn—11 (–, 13) back neck stitches remaining.

SIZE M ONLY: Knit to the first marker, remove marker, place the next 13 front neck stitches on a holder, turn, leaving the remainder of the round unworked. Bind off 3 stitches at the beginning of the next 2 rows, then 4 stitches at the beginning of the following 2 rows—13 stitches.

FUNNEL COLLAR

ALL SIZES: Using the shorter circular needle or double-pointed needles if it's easier for you, pick up and knit 6 (7, 8) Sleeve stitches, k13 (13, 15) stitches from the front neck holder, pick up and knit 6 (7, 8) Sleeve stitches, k11 (13, 13) stitches from the back neck holder—36 (40, 44) stitches. Place marker to indicate the beginning of the round and join.

Work the openwork rib pattern for 20 rounds. Bind off loosely.

FINISHING

Sew the Sleeve seams and underarm seams. Weave in ends.

KEY

☐ K on RS, P on W

⊡ yo

◿ K2tog on RS, P2tog on WS

◺ SSK on RS

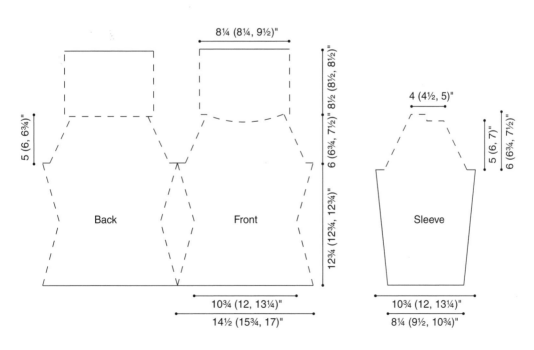

autumn vines scarf

PAGE 46

This scarf's special twist is just that: a pair of front-crossed cables that float like twisted vines along openwork bands made by dropped-stitch ladders. Cables aren't nearly as difficult as they seem; knitting some stitches out of order pulls the material to the left or right, creating the twined effect. Don't be concerned that, as you knit, you aren't making the ladders all along—you'll create them once you've bound off the end of the scarf and undone the dropped stitches.

SIZE
One Size

KNITTED MEASUREMENTS
8" x 56" (20.5cm x 142cm)

MATERIALS

 super bulky

2 hanks Twinkle Handknits Soft Chunky, 100% virgin merino wool, 7 oz/200g, 83 yds/75m, #19 Cream

US size 19 (15mm) needles or size needed to obtain gauge

Cable needle

Tapestry needle

GAUGE
8 stitches = 5" (12.5cm) in stockinette stitch (see page 59)

TAKE THE TIME TO CHECK YOUR GAUGE.

ABBREVIATION
C4L (cable 4 left)—Slip the next 2 stitches to a cable needle and hold in front of the work, k2, k2 from the cable needle.

SCARF

Cast on 12 stitches. Knit 2 rows.

SET-UP ROW (RS): P1, k1, [yo, k4] twice, yo, k1, p1—15 stitches.

ROWS 1 AND 3 (WS): K1, p13, k1.

ROW 2: P1, k2, C4L, k1, C4L, k2, p1.

ROW 4: P1, k13, p1.

Repeat rows 1–4, 26 more times, then rows 1–3 once.

NEXT ROW (RS): K2, [drop the next stitch, k4] twice, drop the next stitch, k2—12 stitches.

Knit 1 row. Bind off. Allow the dropped stitches to ladder down to the corresponding yarn over in the Set-Up Row. Weave in ends.

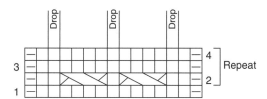

Repeat

KEY

□ K on RS, P on WS

— P on RS, K on WS

⧅ C4L

56"

8"

riverbed shawl PAGE 48

The Riverbed Shawl's sexy curves come from triplets of "knit 2 together" (k2tog) decreases—knitting 2 stitches together as if they were one stitch—worked in succession and followed by yarn overs that yield openings in the knit material. The clustered decreases tug the stripes to and fro, an effect accented by the sway of the extra-long fringe.

SIZE
One Size

KNITTED MEASUREMENTS
15½" x 57" (38.8cm x 145cm)

MATERIALS
 super bulky

3 hanks Twinkle Handknits Soft Chunky, 100% virgin merino wool, 7 oz/200g, 83 yds/75m, #09 Black (A)

2 hanks #06 Baby Pink (B)

US size 19 (15mm) 29" (75cm) circular needle or size needed to obtain gauge

Tapestry needle

Large crochet hook (size P/Q [15mm]) for attaching fringe

GAUGE
8 stitches and 12 rows = 5" (12.5cm) in feather and fan stripes

TAKE THE TIME TO CHECK YOUR GAUGE.

NOTE
A circular needle is used to accommodate the large number of stitches; work back and forth in rows.

FEATHER AND FAN STRIPES
(MULTIPLE OF 18 + 2)

ROW 1 (RS): With A, knit.

ROW 2: Purl.

ROW 3: K1, *k2tog 3 times, [yo, k1] 6 times, k2tog 3 times; repeat from * to last stitch, k1.

ROW 4: Knit.

ROWS 5-8: With B, repeat rows 1–4.

Repeat rows 1–8 for pattern.

SHAWL

With A, cast on 92 stitches. Work in feather and fan stripes until 8 stripes are complete; then work rows 1–4 again. Bind off loosely. Weave in ends.

FRINGE

Cut sixty 26" (66cm) lengths of A and forty-eight 26" (66cm) lengths of B. Matching fringe color to stripe color, attach 3 sets of double-stranded fringe to each end of each stripe (page 60).

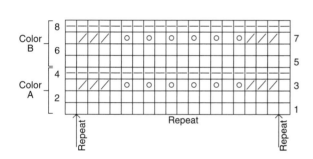

KEY

☐ K on RS, P on WS

◌ yo

╱ K2tog on RS, P2tog on WS

⊟ P on RS, K on WS

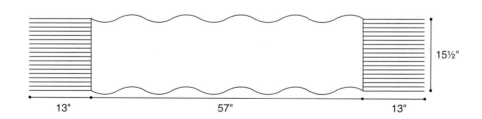

15½"

13"   57"   13"

Create long vertical stripes easily by knitting this scarf the long way. Then cut the blue yarn and keep the white yarn attached in order to knit the stitches you pick up from the ends. Here, you'll work what I call the knot ridge stitch to form the distinctive rows with textured bumps. In the knot ridge stitch, knitting 3 stitches together through the back loops tightly gathers and raises them. The scarf's whimsical end panels also give structure and shape.

arbor row scarf PAGE 50

SIZE
One Size

KNITTED MEASUREMENTS
5" x 90" (12.5cm x 229cm)

MATERIALS

 super bulky

2 hanks Twinkle Handknits Soft Chunky, 100% virgin merino wool, 7 oz/200g, 83 yds/75m, #08 White (A)

1 hank #14 Sapphire (B)

1 hank #10 Kelly Green (C)

US size 19 (15mm) 29" (75cm) circular needle or size needed to obtain gauge

Tapestry needle

GAUGE
8 stitches and 14 rows = 5" (12.5cm) in garter stitch (see page 59)

10 stitches = 5" (12.5cm) and 18 rows = 7" (18cm) in knot ridge stitch on size 19 (15mm) needles

TAKE THE TIME TO CHECK YOUR GAUGE.

ABBREVIATIONS
sl 1 wyib—Slip 1 stitch with yarn in the back.
k3tog-tbl—Knit 3 stitches together through the back loops.

NOTES
A circular needle is used to accommodate the large number of stitches; work back and forth in rows. Carry the color not in use up the side of the work; do not cut it.

KNOT RIDGE STITCH
(MULTIPLE OF 2 + 1)

ROW 1 (RS): With A, knit.

ROW 2: With A, purl.

ROW 3: With C, k1, (k1, yo, k1) in the next stitch, *sl 1 wyib, (k1, yo, k1) in the next stitch; repeat from * to last stitch, k1.

ROW 4: With C, k1, k3tog-tbl, *sl 1 wyib, k3tog-tbl; repeat from * to last stitch, k1.

ROW 5: With A, knit.

ROW 6: With A, purl.

ROW 7: With B, (k1, yo, k1) in the first stitch, *sl 1 wyib, (k1, yo, k1) in the next stitch; repeat from * to end.

ROW 8: With B, k3tog-tbl, *sl 1wyib, k3tog-tbl; repeat from * to end.

Repeat rows 1–8 for pattern.

SCARF
CENTER SECTION

With A, cast on 110 stitches. *With A, knit 2 rows. With B, knit 2 rows. Repeat from * two more times. Cut B. With A, knit 2 rows. Bind off, but do not cut A.

ENDS

With right side facing and using A, pick up 11 stitches along the short edge of the scarf (row 1 of the knot ridge stitch). Beginning with row 2 of the knot ridge stitch, work even until the piece measures approximately 11" (28cm) from the picked-up row, ending with row 2 of the knot ridge stitch. Bind off.

With the right side facing, pick up 11 stitches along the other end and work as for the first end.

FINISHING

Weave in yarn ends.

Reverse stockinette stitch lends a subtle texture to this garment; the garter stitch at the cuffs and bottom hem meshes neatly with the reverse stockinette and prevents the edge from curling. Nearly invisible raglan sleeve shaping yields a cozy fit that focuses attention on the charming flowing ruffle formed with short rows.

cloudburst cardigan

PAGE 52

SIZE
S (M, L)

REMEMBER TO USE THIS GUIDE TO FIND YOUR SIZE BASED ON YOUR ACTUAL BUST MEASUREMENT: S = 34"–36" (86cm–91cm); M = 37"–39" (94cm–99cm); L = 40"–42" (102cm–107cm).

KNITTED MEASUREMENTS
Bust (buttoned): 35½ (38, 40½)" (90 [96.5, 103]cm)

Back length (not including collar): 21 (21, 22)" (53.5 [53.5, 56]cm)

MATERIALS
 super bulky

5 (5, 6) hanks Twinkle Handknits Soft Chunky, 100% virgin merino wool, 7 oz/200g, 83 yds/75m, #27 Urchin

US size 19 (15mm) 24" (61cm) circular needle or size needed to obtain gauge

Stitch holders

Stitch markers

Tapestry needle

Two 1" (2.5cm) buttons

GAUGE
11 stitches and 16 rows = 7" (18cm) in reverse stockinette stitch (see page 59)

TAKE THE TIME TO CHECK YOUR GAUGE.

NOTES
A circular needle is used to accommodate the large number of stitches. The Sleeves are knit first, then the Body. The Sleeves are joined to the Body at the underarms, and the sweater is knit in one piece from that point. The front neckline is formed by short rows.

ABBREVIATIONS
RS Decrease Row—*Purl to 3 stitches before the marker, ssp, p1, slip marker, p1, p2tog; repeat from * 3 times, purl to the end.
WS Decrease Row—*Knit to 3 stitches before the marker, k2tog, k1, slip marker, k1, ssk; repeat from * 3 times, knit to the end.
Reverse Stockinette Stitch—Purl on the right side; knit on the wrong side.

RUFFLE PATTERN

ROW 1 (RS): P5, wrap and turn (1 short row) (page 63).

ROW 2 AND ALL WS ROWS: Knit.

ROW 3: P3, wrap and turn (1 short row).

ROW 5: Purl, picking up the wraps.

ROW 7: Purl.

ROWS 9-12: Repeat rows 1–4 (2 short rows).

ROW 13: Purl.

ROW 14: Knit.

Repeat rows 1–14 for pattern.

LEFT SLEEVE

Cast on 19 (21, 23) stitches. Knit 4 rows (2 ridges).

Change to reverse stockinette stitch and work even until the Sleeve measures approximately 13½ (14, 14½)" (34.5 [35.5, 37]cm), ending with a wrong-side (knit) row.

UNDERARM SHAPING

Bind off 2 stitches at the beginning of the next row and 1 stitch at the beginning of the following row. Place the remaining 16 (18, 20) stitches on a holder.

RIGHT SLEEVE

Work as for the Left Sleeve up to the underarm shaping step.

UNDERARM SHAPING

Bind off 1 stitch at the beginning of the next row and 2 stitches at the beginning of the following row. Place the remaining 16 (18, 20) stitches on a holder.

BODY

Cast on 17 (18, 19) stitches, place marker to indicate the right underarm, cast on 28 (30, 32) stitches, place marker to indicate the left underarm, cast on 16 (17, 18) stitches—61 (65, 69) stitches. Knit 4 rows (2 ridges).

NEXT ROW (RS): Purl to last 2 stitches, k2.

Keeping 2 stitches at the left front edge in garter stitch and the remainder of the stitches in reverse stockinette stitch, work even until the Body measures approximately 13 (13, 13)" (33 [33, 33]cm) from the beginning, ending with a right-side row.

DIVIDE THE BODY

NEXT ROW (WS): Removing the markers as you work, ★knit to 1 stitch before the marker, bind off 2 stitches; repeat from ★ once, knit to the end—57 (61, 65) stitches remain.

JOIN THE SLEEVES AND BODY

NEXT ROW (RS): P16 (17, 18), place marker for the raglan shaping, p16 (18, 20) Right Sleeve stitches from holder, place marker for the raglan shaping, p26 (28, 30) back stitches, place marker for the raglan shaping, p16 (18, 20) Left Sleeve stitches from holder, place marker for the raglan shaping, p13 (14, 15), k2—89 (97, 105) stitches. Knit 1 row.

RAGLAN SHAPING, NECK SHAPING, AND BUTTONHOLES

NOTE: READ ALL INSTRUCTIONS IN THIS SECTION BEFORE BEGINNING. MANY ACTIONS ARE TAKING PLACE AT THE SAME TIME.

Keeping 2 stitches at the left front edge in garter stitch, work Decrease Row on the next row, then every 3 rows 3 (3, 1) more time(s), then every other row 1 (2, 5) time(s), working RS or WS Decrease Rows as appropriate—49 (49, 49) stitches remain.

SIZE S ONLY: Work 1 row even.

NEXT ROW: Decrease on the front and back stitches only—45 stitches. Work 1 row even; repeat Decrease Row once—37 stitches remain.

SIZE M ONLY: Work 1 row even.

NEXT ROW: Work Decrease Row, omitting the decreases at the Front Sleeve edges—43 stitches remain. Work 1 row even.

NEXT ROW: Decrease on the front and back stitches only—39 stitches remain.

SIZE L ONLY: ★Work 1 row even.

NEXT ROW: Decrease on the front and back stitches only—45 stitches remain; repeat from ★ once—41 stitches remain.

ALL SIZES: *At the same time,* when 6 (6, 8) rows of raglan shaping are complete, work the buttonhole row at the right front edge as follows:

BUTTONHOLE ROW (RS): P2, yo, p2tog; work in established pattern to end.

Work in pattern for 9 more rows; repeat the buttonhole row.

At the same time, when 12 (13, 14) rows of raglan shaping are complete, work short rows as follows, maintaining the raglan shaping:

Work to 4 stitches from the left front edge, wrap and turn; work to 5 stitches from the right front edge, wrap and turn; work to 6 stitches from the left front edge, wrap and turn; work to 7 stitches from the right front edge, wrap and turn. Continue on all stitches, picking up all wraps—37 (39, 41) stitches remain when all shaping is complete. Knit 5 rows for the collar. Bind off loosely.

RUFFLE

Cast on 7 stitches. Work 2 (2, 4) rows in reverse stockinette stitch. Work 7 full (14-row) repeats of the ruffle pattern, then 2 (2, 4) rows in reverse stockinette stitch. Bind off.

FINISHING

Sew the Sleeve and underarm seams. Sew the Ruffle to the right front edge. Weave in ends.

Laying the cardigan closed at the front, mark the positions of the buttons using the following guide: Place the first button on the 8th stitch in from the opening edge and on the 10th row down from the neckline edge. Place the second button on the 6th stitch in from the opening edge and on the 18th row down from the neckline edge. (The Ruffle's weight requires you to situate the buttons higher than usual, so the buttons may seem misaligned until you put on the sweater.) Sew on the buttons, creating shanks, if necessary, to accommodate the thickness of the knit fabric.

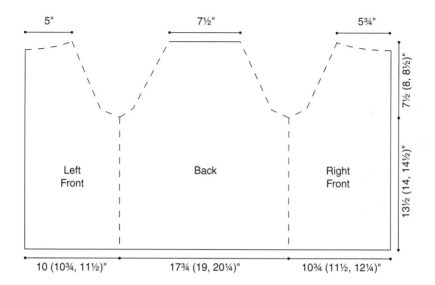

5"

7½"

5¾"

Left
Front

Back

Right
Front

7½ (8, 8½)"

13½ (14, 14½)"

10 (10¾, 11½)"

17¾ (19, 20¼)"

10¾ (11½, 12¼)"

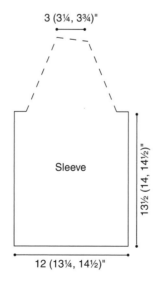

3 (3¼, 3¾)"

Sleeve

13½ (14, 14½)"

12 (13¼, 14½)"

meridian tunic dress

PAGE 54

Nothing knits up faster than a stockinette project worked on circular needles. This garment's narrow rib band at the neckline and armholes and on the straps adds structure and elasticity along with a little subtle detailing. Its body-hugging dimensions through the chest and at the underarms ensure modesty. The yarn's lustrous (and breathable) silk-and-cotton blend makes this a perfect summer-weight tog.

SIZE
XS (S, M, L)

REMEMBER TO USE THIS GUIDE TO FIND YOUR SIZE BASED ON YOUR ACTUAL BUST MEASUREMENT: XS = 31"–33" (79cm–84cm); S = 34"–36" (86cm–91cm); M = 37"–39" (94cm–99cm); L = 40"–42" (102cm–107cm).

KNITTED MEASUREMENTS
Bust 29 (30½, 32, 33½)" (73.5 [77.5, 81.5, 85]cm)

MATERIALS

 fine

5 (5, 6, 6) balls Twinkle Handknits Cruise, 70% silk/30% cotton, 3½ oz/50g, 120 yds/109m, #09 Black (A)

3 (3, 4, 4) skeins #08 White (B)

2 (2, 2, 2) skeins #24 Lavender (C)

US size 15 (10mm) 24" (60cm) circular needle or size needed to obtain gauge

US size 11 (8mm) 24" (60cm) circular needle

Stitch markers

Stitch holders

Tapestry needle

GAUGE
10 stitches and 12 rnds = 4" (10cm) in stockinette stitch (see page 59) with 4 strands held together

TAKE THE TIME TO CHECK YOUR GAUGE.

ABBREVIATION
Inc 1—knit 1 in the row below the next stitch, knit the next stitch.

NOTES
The dress is knit in the round. The stitch marker at the beginning of the round should be a different color from the others. The entire piece is worked in stockinette stitch with 4 strands held together, then turned inside out to use the wrong side as the right side. Weave in ends on the knit side of the fabric.

DRESS

With 4 strands of A held together, cast on 40 (40, 44, 44) stitches, place marker to indicate the side, cast on 40 (40, 44, 44) stitches, place marker to indicate the beginning of the round—80 (80, 88, 88) stitches. Join, being careful not to twist stitches.

RNDS 1-10: *K4, p4; repeat from * around.

RND 11, SIZE XS ONLY: With B, *k18, k2tog; repeat from * 3 times—76 stitches.

RND 11, SIZES S AND L ONLY: With B, knit.

RND 11, SIZE M ONLY With B, *k20, k2tog; repeat from * 3 times—84 stitches.

RNDS 12-19, ALL SIZES: With B, knit.

RNDS 20-28: With A, knit.

RND 29 (DECREASE RND): With C, *k1, ssk, knit to 3 stitches before the marker; k2tog, k1; repeat from * once more—72 (76, 80, 84) stitches.

RNDS 30-37: With C, knit.

RNDS 38-45: With A, knit.

RND 46: With A, repeat Decrease Rnd—68 (72, 76, 80) stitches.

RNDS 47-51: With B, knit.

RND 52 (INCREASE RND): With B, *k1, inc 1, knit to 2 stitches before the marker, inc 1, k1; repeat from * once more—72 (76, 80, 84) stitches.

RNDS 53-55: With B, knit.

RNDS 56-57: With A, knit.

RND 58: With A, knit to 2 stitches before the beginning-of-round marker.

DIVIDE FOR ARMHOLES

Removing markers as you work, bind off 4 stitches, knit to 2 stitches before the marker and place these front stitches on a holder, bind off 4 stitches, knit to end—32 (34, 36, 38) back stitches remain.

SHAPE BACK ARMHOLES AND NECK

NOTE: CHANGE TO C WHEN REQUIRED TO MAINTAIN THE STRIPING PATTERN.

Working back and forth, bind off 1 stitch at the beginning of the next 6 rows—26 (28, 30, 32) stitches. Work even for 1 (1, 3, 5) rows.

NEXT ROW (RS): K9, place the next 8 (10, 12, 14) stitches on a holder, join another ball of yarn and knit to end.

Working both sides at once with separate balls of yarn, bind off 2 stitches at each neck edge 3 times—3 stitches remain on each side. Bind off.

SHAPE FRONT ARMHOLES AND NECK

Place front stitches onto a needle and work as for the back.

BACK NECK BAND

Turn the body inside out so that the right side (purl side) is facing.

With the right side facing, using B and beginning at the back right shoulder, pick up and knit 10 stitches along the back neck edge, knit 8 (10, 12, 14) stitches from the holder, pick up and knit 10 stitches to the shoulder—28 (30, 32, 34) stitches.

ROW 1 (WS): K0 (1, 2, 3), p4, *k4, p4; repeat from * to last 0 (1, 2, 3) stitches, k0 (1, 2, 3).

ROW 2: P0 (1, 2, 3), k4, *p4, k4; repeat from * to last 0 (1, 2, 3) stitches, p0 (1, 2, 3).

ROW 3: Repeat row 1.

Bind off in rib.

FRONT NECK BAND

Work as for the Back Neck Band.

LEFT ARM BAND

With the right side facing, using B and beginning at the left underarm edge, pick up and knit 16 (16, 18, 18) stitches along the front armhole edge, cast on 16 (16, 18, 18) stitches, pick up and knit 16 stitches along the back armhole edge, place marker to indicate the beginning of the round—48 (48, 56, 56) stitches.

ROW 1 (WS): K2, *p4, k4; repeat from * to last 6 stitches, p4, k2.

ROW 2: P2tog, *k4, p4; repeat from * to last 6 stitches, k4, p2—47 (47, 55, 55) stitches.

ROW 3: K2tog, *p4, k4; repeat from * to last 5 stitches, p4, k1—46 (46, 54, 54) stitches.
Bind off in rib.

RIGHT ARM BAND

Work as for the Left Arm Band, picking up stitches along the back armhole edge first.

FINISHING

Sew underarm seam on Arm Bands.
Weave in ends.

TWINKLE KNIT BIT
KEEP A NOTEPAD OR A ROW COUNTER AT HAND TO TALLY STITCHES OR ROWS AS YOU KNIT THEM. OR USE A HIGHLIGHTER MARKER TO CHECK OFF LINES IN YOUR PATTERN AS YOU COMPLETE THEM.

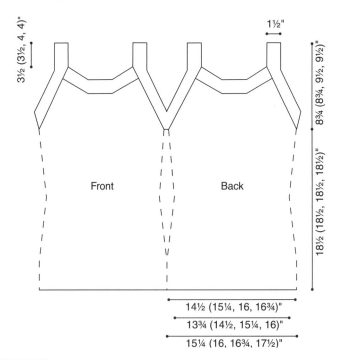

YARN RESOURCES AND SUBSTITUTION

Along with the sweaters in this book, I've designed the yarns they're worked in. Soft Chunky, Kids Mohair, and Cruise were created to deliver the look and feel I wanted in my designs. For the best results—the perfect shape, the perfect drape, the perfect fit, and the right amount of give—I suggest you use the specific yarns called for in the patterns. Twinkle yarns are sold at fine yarn stores everywhere. Check the website www.classiceliteyarns.com to find the store nearest you.

However, if you want to substitute a different yarn for Twinkle Handknits, be sure the fiber content, gauge, and overall yarn characteristics are the same. Below are suggestions for yarns that have a gauge and fiber content similar to the ones used. Please keep in mind that I have not tested these yarns myself, and they may create a sweater different in look and feel from the one pictured.

For Soft Chunky, try: **6**
Magnum from Cascade
Bulky Lopi from JCA
Baby from Tahki Stacy Charles

When substituting for Kids Mohair and Cruise, you may need to experiment with the number of strands needed to meet the gauge.

For Kids Mohair, try: **2**
Lace Mohair from Karabella
Baby Kid Extra from Filatura di Crosa, distributed by Tahki Stacy Charles

For Cruise, try: **2**
Cotton Bamboo from Classic Elite Yarns
Cotton Fine from Brown Sheep Company
Breeze from Crystal Palace

STANDARD YARN WEIGHT SYSTEM

YARN WEIGHT SYMBOL AND CATEGORY NAMES	**2** FINE	**6** SUPER BULKY
TYPES OF YARN IN CATEGORY	SPORT, BABY	BULKY, ROVING
KNIT GAUGE RANGE* IN STOCKINETTE STITCH TO 4 INCHES (10 CM)	23–26 sts	6–11 sts
RECOMMENDED NEEDLE IN METRIC SIZE RANGE	3.25–3.75 mm	8 mm and larger
RECOMMENDED NEEDLE IN U.S. SIZE RANGE	3 to 5	11 and larger

ABOUT THE AUTHOR

Wenlan Chia is the founder and designer of the fashion label Twinkle by Wenlan. Born in Taiwan, she emigrated to the United States when she was twenty-three.

Twinkle launched in 1999 with an array of colorful, exuberant chunky-knit sweaters, which have become Wenlan's signature. The world of Twinkle has grown to include Twinkle Handknit Yarn, a line of home products named Twinkle Living, Twinkle Accessories, and a fine jewelry collection called Twinkle Jewels.

The Twinkle collection has been featured in publications including *Elle, Harper's Bazaar, InStyle,* the *New York Times,* and *Vogue,* among others. Wenlan has received prestigious awards such as the Onward Kashiyama New Design Prize in Tokyo and the Competition of Young Fashion Designers in Paris.

Wenlan currently resides in New York City with her husband, Bernard, and her French bulldog, Milan. Her first book was *Twinkle's Big City Knits.*

INDEX

A
abbreviations, 65
Arbor Row Scarf, 50–51, **116–117**
Autumn Vines Scarf, 46–47,
    112–113

B
Borealis Sweater, 36–37, **88–90**
Boysenberry Scarf, 20–21, **68–69**
buttonholes, 60

C
chunky yarn, 58
circular needles, 57
    garter stitch on, 59
    reverse stockinette stitch on,
    59
    stockinette stitch on, 59
Cloudburst Cardigan, 52–53,
    118–121

D
decreases, 60
Dress, Meridian Tunic, 54–55,
    122–124

E
Equator iPod Sleeve, 38–39, **98–99**

F
Friday Night collection, 18–31,
    68–81
fringe, 60, **69**, 70

G
garter stitch, 59
gauge, 58

H
Hanger Covers, 30–31, **80–81**
Hats
    Snowcap, 34–35, **84–85**
    Urchin Beret, 40–41, **104–105**
Horizon Tunic, 24–25, **72–74**

I
increases, 60
iPod Sleeve, 38–39, **98–99**

J
joining stitches, 60

K
K1, p1 rib, 59
K2, p2 rib, 59

L
Lilac Mist Throw, 28–29, **78–79**

M
markers, 61
Meridian Tunic Dress, 54–55,
    122–124

N
Nightfall Cropped Top, 26–27,
    75–77
Nimbus Sweater, 16–17, 44–45,
    108–111
Northern Cross Sweater, 16,
    40–41, **100–103**

O
Oceania Sweater, 38–39, **94–97**

P
Peony Scarf, 34–35, **86–87**
picking up stitches, 61
preparation tips, 57

R
reverse stockinette stitch, 59
Riverbed Shawl, 48–49, **114–115**

S
Sand Dune Hanger Covers, 30–31,
    80–81
Saturday Morning collection,
32–41
Scarves
    Arbor Row, 50–51, **116–117**
    Autumn Vines, 46–47, **112–113**
    Boysenberry, 20–21, **68–69**
    Peony, 34–35, **86–87**
    Wisteria, 22–23, **70–71**
seaming, 62
seed stitch, 59

sewing, 62
short rows, 63
Snowcap Hat, 34–35, **84–85**
stitch holders, 63
stitches, 59
stockinette stitch, 59
Sunday Afternoon collection,
    42–55, **108–125**
Sweaters
    Borealis, 36–37, **88–90**
    Cloudburst Cardigan, 52–53
    Nimbus, 16–17, 44–45, **108–111**
    Northern Cross, 16, 40–41,
    100–103
    Oceania, 38–39, **94–97**
    Tidepool, 38–39, **91–93**

T
three-needle bind-off, 63
Tidepool Sweater, 38–39, **91–93**
Tops
    Borealis Sweater, 36–37, **88–90**
    Cloudburst Cardigan, 52–53,
    118–121
    Horizon Tunic, 24–25, **72–74**
    Nightfall Cropped Top, 26–27,
    75–77
    Oceania Sweater, 38–39, **94–97**
    Tidepool Sweater, 38–39
triple-knotted fringe, **69**

U
Urchin Beret, 40–41, **104–105**

W
Wisteria Scarf, 22–23, **70–71**
Wraps
    Lilac Mist Throw, 28–29, **78–79**
    Riverbed Shawl, 48–49, **114–115**

Y
yarns, 58